Yellowbird

YELLOWBIRD

by
Judy R. Smith

Lewis-Clark Press
Lewiston, ID

Published by:
Lewis-Clark Press
Kimberly Verhines, Series Editor
1437 Burrell Ave
Lewiston, ID   83501
lcpublishing@hotmail.com

ISBN: 0-911015-59-0
978-0-911015-59-1

Cover art: "Swallowing Her Intuition," oil on canvas, by Ellen Vieth
Artwork used by courtesy of Ellen Vieth

Book design by Mark Sanders

Manufactured in the United States of America

For John and Pitty, resting souls.

Author's Preface:

Sophia Peabody Hawthorne is drawn in part from biographical history; she is partly fictional.

Lizzie Shaw Melville is hardly drawn from biographical history; she is mostly fictional.

Yellowbird is not drawn at all from biographical history; she is completely fictional.

-Yellowbird-

Yellowbird lives in such a well-hidden grove that no one has found it. She is old; she is frail. She dresses in rawhide and has been weaving for thousands of years. Her quills are a rainbow of deep, rich hues. She has dyed some with walnuts, others with blueberries, still others with choke cherry or bloodroot. She has bitten off the barbed ends of so many porcupine quills that her teeth are worn to smooth little mounds. A huge motley dog stays at her side, intent on the blanket she is weaving, has been weaving these thousands of years.

A few yards away is a large fire that has been burning for thousands of years. Above it hangs a huge iron pot filled with the root and berry stew she loves so well. Her soup has simmered for thousands of years. No matter how much Yellowbird eats or uses, the pot never empties.

When Yellowbird rises to stir the pot, Motley Dog pulls out quills from the blanket. She pulls out many because Yellowbird is so old and so frail that it takes her many hours to walk between the pot and the blanket. So Yellowbird begins again to weave, always having to replace what Motley Dog undoes, never able to finish the intricate pattern of the blanket she is weaving, has been weaving these thousand of years.

The old-timers say that if Yellowbird ever finishes the blanket the world will come to an end. — Lulu Hawkridge Hitchcock

"A man with true, warm heart, and a soul and an intellect,—with life to his fingertips; earnest, sincere, and reverent; very tender and modest. And I am not sure that he is not a very great man. He has very keen perceptive power; but what astonishes me is, that his eyes are not large and deep. He seems to me to see everything accurately; and how he can do so with his small eyes, I cannot tell. They are not keen eyes, either, but quite undistinguished in any way. His nose is straight and handsome, his mouth expressive of sensibility and emotion. He is tall and erect, with an air free, brave, and manly. When conversing, he is full of gesture and force, and loses himself in his subject. There is no grace or polish. Once in a while, his animation gives place to a singularly quiet expression, out of those eyes to which I have objected; an indrawn, dim look, but which at the same time makes you feel that he is at that instant taking deepest note of what is before him. It is a strange, lazy glance, but with a power in it quite unique. It does not seem to penetrate through you, but to take you into itself." — *Sophia Peabody Hawthorne, describing Herman Melville, in a letter to her mother*

You always said, mother, to let you know when I met the right one. Well, neither may be the right one but the two of them sure are uncommon. Down at the pier, hearing the waves lap at us so. The way they devour the sand that supports them, smooth it to nothing as they slam and slam and slam. Still gives me chills, small as it is. It's got a god-damned barb on its tip, I say to the first one. Just like an old tomcat, I say. Like a damned harpoon, I tell him. Very like a harpoon, he laughs, feebly. Why the hell else does the she-cat turn and tear? I hiss. And I tell the other one the same thing. I know better than to marry. I'm not sand. — Lizzie Shaw Melville, she imagined

Lizzie

I do not wonder why it has come to me to do this. I am older now, but memory holds. I did not heed my own warning; I married. I became sand. But sand can speak even from its beaten smoothness. I will escape him, whole and strong, I swear.

I remember Louisa Alcott. Writing did not save her. She has visions. She thinks her house has no roof; she dreams that figures come from the sky and assault her. She thinks she is married to a dark-skinned Spaniard. Dressed in black velvet, he stands before her, commanding her to lie low, and very still, and very silent. She sees his black-gloved hand; she feels its weight.

Sophia told me that she wrote a great deal and always kept what she wrote in her sewing chest. She told Hawthorne but he never read any of it. Herman always tried to find mine, no matter how deeply I hid them.

I wrote pieces—just pieces and kept them in many places. He did not find them all, make them whole.

I have saved myself. From these scattered fragments, I will now emerge. I will escape him: that is my grace. My great-grandmother Lulu is with me. I imagine her face next to mine, her hands around my waist, soft and smooth as the sky.

Sophia

I saw the face and shoulders of a man, a handsome man, a man handsome in a most unusual manner. He was truncated at the middle of the chest rather than at the waist. This figure had deeply piercing dark black eyes that seemed not to belong to a man at all. I'll call them feminine eyes because I don't know what else to call them. They gazed at me with a powerful, animate force that nearly fixed me to the spot. His eyes were painted with such a successive series of circular strokes, as I must call them, that to stare into them gave you the sensation of looking into dark, reflective glass, of being carried into a whirlpool except that you were not anywhere in or near the sea.

Perhaps it was the odd and unsettling frame. The landscape of the canvas was virtually bereft of the usual anchors. I have mixed my metaphors, I know, but I have long felt the land and the sea are one. No visible chair, no book in arms. The figure literally seemed to float. The fluid motion of this, however, was abruptly halted by the frame, full three-inches wide, one of those elaborately carved and gilded ones, heavy and rigid in its mass. So there was this floating figure encased, leaving you to ponder the significance of it all, if significance there is.

I shake whenever I remember just how that portrait looks at me— even now. It riveted me to the spot then and I keep returning to it, turning over in my mind what must be behind those blue-black eyes, eyes so black-blue that the contrast between them and the pallor of the skin seems oddly expected, oddly congruous. I don't know whether it was the artist or not, but whoever framed it clipped the figure severely. The frame is not unlike the cravat. Its full paislied folds, so apparently full and flowing and yet so restricting, so rigid, as if it is trying to hold in whatever force in his mind has made the hair wave on end. His hair radiates outward—though in no symmetrical pattern—so that it connects him to some space only hinted at within the portrait and not contained by the frame, despite its ponderous weight. There's a strange smile—if smile it even is—that taunts you, confuses you. It seems as if he is about to speak but without sound.

Lizzie

My cousin loved to tell this story. We all call her Pecker. She wasn't born Pecker, but, as she put it, she finally got enough sense to know that that's who she was. Her birth name was Dentitia (from a woman her mother had heard about who kept tied in a ribbon around her ankle what she swore was the tooth she'd been born with and which the doctor said made her a terrible thing to have to nurse) Hermione (from her grandmother who had gotten it from her mother who had read it somewhere) Stanford (from her grandfather) Melville, but, as usual, what others gave you never fit. So she changed and gave herself Pecker, just plain Pecker, first and last, because she was the only one who knew enough to do it.

Pecker always knew there was something different about her and that it came from the memory of what her mother had done. Dead when Pecker was but three, her grandmother—Flora Harrington—taught Pecker all she ever needed to know about the difference between men and women. And between those foreigners and us. The French Catholics, who moved across the Canadian border adjoining Pecker's northern Vermont home, moved slowly at first, staying away from the town center, living on its outskirts. But they kept coming and coming and they talked together in a language nobody else understood. They came into the middle of town, erasing the borders, showing their dark, foreign faces in the middle of the day in the middle of the town.

And then they started doing it, like there was nothing wrong at all. Right out in the open where even children could see them. They took the arms of white, Protestant, God-fearing women and walked them right down the center of town. And then they built their church. Nobody stopped them. They were afraid to—afraid of a tribe they heard chanting in the fields at night. Those French men held strange rites and they held them with women, three or four at a time, pounding them full of the devil's religion. And when Flora Harrington told Pecker the story, it was enough to make even her believe devils walked the earth once more. And it was because of womanly parts, Flora said,—they were what was and always would be the thing that drew the devil out and let him loose in the night.

13

So when Sarah Melville walked into their fields night after night, her husband knew he had to bring her home. Armed with his faith in the Lord and the words of God in his mouth, he left to bring her back from the hell-services in the open fields of the night. But Jeremiah lost faith that night. Sarah was gone but Jeremiah lay on the ground next to a scythe. His legs spread open around it, the curve of the blade resting in the space that used to be his crotch. Those who found him knew they faced a fearsome power. Those devils had buried his rod, but left the rest of him unburied. Jeremiah, crotchless, faced his maker. It put silence and religion into everybody, so Flora said.

And then she told the story of her uncle Buster Harrington and his sick wife. Ruth had been out helping Buster with the plowing—which she had to do because there wasn't enough money to hire hands which she said was always ridiculous anyway because if you'd get just the hands it would be all right but you always got the whole body to feed along with it—and she just fell flat on the ground. Dead three days later. The doctor was baffled. But Buster wasn't. The way he'd shake his head, you just knew he had a deep and solemn knowledge of unearthly things.

Pecker's father, Hiram, had never gotten along very well with his half-brother Buster. Hiram always said that Buster knew enough not to say anything until it was too late and then people had to help him no matter how much they didn't want to. Would feel eternally guilty if they didn't. Like the time Buster and Ruth came to visit one summer. They came over on the train and stayed two weeks, telling about how well things were going. Taking Hiram and his wife Penelope out to dinner and buying expensive things.

Then it was time to go home. But when it was time to get to the station Buster and Ruth just sat there like there wasn't any need to get up ever. Hiram said, "Come on, now, time's getting short." But Buster and Ruth still sat. So Hiram said, "Come on, now, otherwise we'll miss the train."

"Well, I reckon it don't make no difference whether we miss the train or not," Buster whispered.

14

Hiram put down the bag he had just picked up and said "What the hell you mean? Course it makes a difference."

"You're wrong there, Hiram," and Buster put his head down even further as he continued, "it don't make no difference at all."

"Why the hell not?"

"'Cause we ain't taking the train."

Hiram forced himself to wait before he asked, "Well, then, how the hell you getting home? It's too far to walk and I don't know of any horses and wagon you suddenly got hold of and I don't have none you can borrow."

Buster licked his teeth. "You're right there, Hiram. Is too far to walk. And nope, ain't got no horse or wagon neither."

"Then what the hell you mean when you say that you ain't taking no train?"

Buster picked up his head. "Well, now, you see we's anxious to go and you's anxious to have us go, but it's too far to walk and we ain't got no horse or wagon neither, and you can't lend us the only one you got, what with you needin' it for the farm and all, and since we ain't takin' no train, that makes things kind of strange, now don't it? We want to get there, but there don't seem to be no way of us goin'."

Hiram was angry, confused. "You goddamn fool, why ain't you taking the train?"

Buster lifted his head higher. "'Cause we ain't got no tickets."

"For Christ's sake, you buy your goddamned tickets at the station. What the hell you think the station's for?"

"Can't do that, I'm afraid."

"And why the hell not?"

Buster lifted his head full up. "Well, it's 'cause me and Ruth here ain't got no more money. We spent it all. On you, of course."

None of them should have been surprised either by Buster's account of the last night Ruth walked the earth. He believed in ghosts—especially the ones who came into Ruth in the field that day and took her. Penetrated her and left her. Filled her with morbid excitement as they entered her, pressing her spine into the earth.

Sophia

It was in Cuba that I felt it first. In Cuba. On horseback. Out horse-back riding, hatless, hair radiating outward, feeling the wind crash into me, over me, around me as I sliced into it, galloping into the sky that wasn't just sky but joined to the earth, galloping into it, gathered close with blue-black shapes changing and shifting as I drove, unsheeted, to the soul's wind. They handed me off the horse. It was there, then, that I understood ecstasy is a shape of a thing rather than a thing itself, a thing that shapes itself to your shapes and that shapes you to yourself. I'd ride high, hatless, hair-spoked wheel of my own circumference.

And then again, at the bottom of the stairs of that old Salem house. Those blue-black eyes looked up, unhatted me, put me back on that Cuban horse, radiated shape into space and galloped into the clouds, gathering stormy and potent in the East.

It is clear to me that I am particularly fond of shapes—and especially of radiated ones. But I cannot find it in my heart to be otherwise. So, yes, I love the very shape that radiates from this very page. And I do not think you can blame me. I know that I use too many modifiers. And repetitions. I hope you do not blame me.

Lizzie

Aunt Gracie scandalized the community by refusing to wear mourning for the year. She said it was ridiculous to assume that an outward show of something had anything to do with what was inside. As she put it, it was plum nonsense to go around looking like a black widow when she wasn't one.

I understood why my mother wore black to her mother's funeral but came home and wore her red bonnet inside the house for the rest of the day. I wonder what her face looked like that night when she undressed herself. Did she stand naked to the wind?

I smile when I remember what Aunt Gracie said when I told her that when Melville visited again I was going to arm myself with a particularly pungent flower so that the sight of me would be one with the smell of me. But Gracie shook her head and laughed. When she laughed she actually yawned, open-mouthed, like a bird waiting for its food. For a moment all you could see was a gaping hole. "You needn't to bother, Lizzie, my girl." She grasped my arm, drew me close and whispered: "It's not in his mind's eye you want to be to begin with. It's in his eye itself. Don't settle, girl, for him being satisfied with his image of you. It's the you in your mind's eye that you want to fuse his smelling soul to."

Sophia

Peas, prunes, prisms. Over and over again. Peas, prunes, prisms. Prisms, prunes, peas. Over and over again you said these. Endless repetition. To keep your mouth small. I will name my first-born Una. U-N-AAAA. By God, she'll open her mouth so wide she'll reveal her naked self, hatless, astride and akimbo that muscular back, uncorseted, moving free into the wind.

He wrote me once that he was sure he could be a painter but he couldn't handle a brush. I wondered how he could be so sure that he couldn't handle a brush and why he would say this to me who was and could.

Mother says that to survive marriage you must become unwell, at least publicly. I am not unwell and I will not be unwell, privately at least.

Lizzie

I am afraid not to marry him now.

I don't love him and I don't hate him but I do feel this awful terror when I am not with him and an even worse horror when I am. I know I don't want to marry him.

When I told him so his eyes narrowed to a slit. Herman stared—a hard, unblinking stare—until I had to lower my head. I couldn't stand his gaze.

"Don't you ever, ever, say no to me again," he snarled.

I said nothing.

"Do you understand me?" he shouted as he grabbed me.

I shook my head. He shook me.

"If you ever say no to me again, I'll split you in two, goddamned you," he spit.

-Yellowbird-

Thousands of years ago, when Yellowbird was young, she dreamed a dream that lasted many, many days. Turtle had been feeling a tingling down his back and imagined that some invisible hand was cutting symbols into his shell. He imagined that there was a mirror image of something carved on each half of his back. He wished there was some way for him to see his back but knew that there was none. So he walked even more slowly than usual, anxious to take time to imagine what he carried.

The tingling suddenly stopped and Turtle instinctively looked above him. His shell broke in two and he fell through the hole that had opened at his feet. He fell for days on end, landing in a huge field through the middle of which ran a river. It didn't hurt. He just opened up and fell, finding himself in a field, near the water. He tingled again and in no time at all a new shell appeared on his back, thick and shiny and strong. When he looked down, he saw the two pieces of his shell that had fallen with him. On it, in mirror images, were strange markings that resembled eyes and claws and teeth. Turtle could not make any sense out of these things so he walked away, happy with his new shell, forgetting the old one that had shown him a new world.

When she woke up, Yellowbird knew that she had seen the beginnings and the endings of all things. The day would come, Yellowbird would say, when Turtle would wish he had watched his back more closely, had paid better attention to the place where earth and water meet the sky.

Sophia

There is one tooth that I keep thinking about; it is father's most unusual specimen. Dentists like to keep such things around, you know. It—rather they—are a large molar, occupying the breadth of two normally-sized ones. And yet, curiously, the roots are completely separate. Father said that it baffled his science; he could find no explanation for it. Roots intertwined, yes, but separate? Damnedest thing, he laughed. I felt and shared the fascinated thrill with which he preserved and observed this phenomenon.

I have spent a lot of time lately doing what almost every other person in town is doing. There is nothing short of a fervor for doing Berlin work. We are fortunate to have so many people here travel abroad regularly and bring home beautifully dyed wool threads with which we can create elaborately detailed pictures on canvases created from a square filled with a grid of holes. The usual way of filling these tiny holes—and thereby creating the picture—is to count one stitch per hole. But I have been doing something less common of late. I am making a bag to carry when I walk abroad. But instead of using wool I am using beads, tiny, tiny beads, of varied hues both bold and pastel and some of the darkest jet, strung on extremely fine thread, so fine that three times as many stitches are needed to fill each hole. I have been working fervently for months now and have but half of one side of the bag formed.

But I can envision the whole plainly. The front side is divided into three areas, each set off by a beaded band of flowers—tiny roses and lilies. Each of these bands is framed by a saw-tooth pattern, so that the hard angular lines add interest to the softer shapes of the worked flowers. The flowers are of pinks, reds and whites; the saw-tooth edge is black and white. In the top space, which occupies only about a quarter of its length, is a basket, out of which spills roses and daisies, some of which have nearly fallen to the saw-toothed floor. In the middle section, which is over half of the entire length, there has begun to appear a sculpted figure of a parrot on a field of branches heavy with fruit. What I have done is to work the bird in reed stitch. Some call it raised stitch but I do not. I have worked that separately, in wool. And then I have taken my stringed beads and woven them through the branches and around the entire figure of the bird and then attached it to the canvas in the center of a cluster of fruit emerging downward from the invisible perch on which the parrot rests. This dimensional wool bird thus rises from its beaded frame in a manner that hides its manner of attachment, creating the illusion that it is free to spread its blue, plumed wings and squawk itself into flight. In the last space, which is not quite a quarter of the entire length, I will bead the date in the brightest of yellows and purples. The back side will be done all in beads of the deepest jet. But the beads will not be set in a simple, straight-lined pattern. They will zigzag over the entire length. I love to feel the rough warmth of the wool rise out of the cool smooth of the beads.

Mother talks of nothing but religion, of angels and death and resurrection and hell. I think of death and illness often, too—the headaches do come so often and sometimes the pain is terribly difficult to endure. And I can barely sleep many nights. Instead of sleep, I have an endlessly revolving palette of visions and colors and shapes that are inside my head and outside on the walls and ceiling of the room. But I am tired of religion and find that it does nothing to stop the shapes that swirl inside and out and that sigh-breathe in and out of me.

Lizzie

I thought the bastard was going to kill me for sure when he found the moccasins. I had not been honest, I know; I had not told him about great-great grandmother. I never knew her—I only know her from the few stories my grandmother used to tell. Mother never spoke of her. But I do have these moccasins. Grandmother gave them to me before she died so mother couldn't throw them away.

They are fine moccasins, the kind used only for rare ceremonial occasions. They are hardly worn; the intricate quillwork is all intact. The colors are not garish; they are the rich, deep, vibrant tones of the earth and sky. They were done before trading started with the whites. The work is so fine that I wonder whether she made them for her marriage ceremony.

I know that she married a white man—John Hawkridge Hitchcock—took the name of Lulu and that they lived in the Saskatchewan Territory where he was a government trapper and hunter. He saw her, loved her at first glance, and bought her for a year's supply of meat and hides. To be bought made her special; it was a rare honor for her and her family. John loved her, doted on her, made Lulu Hawkridge Hitchcock the most precious thing on earth.

He had just returned from checking his traps and had a hard time making it back to the cabin. The snow had come so furiously all morning that he and his horse sank knee-deep. As he sheltered Jackpot, his horse, he thought that they might not make it out for a week or more. Later that evening, Lulu went into labor with their first born. Things soured quickly. The mid-wife, who had traveled some twenty miles to be with her, told John he must go try to find some help. John set out, on snowshoes, to try to find his way to the nearest Settlement, twenty miles away. He was gone for four days but returned with a doctor. Lulu died but the child —a blond haired, hazel-eyed girl—lived.

They said you could hear John's bellows of grief in the Settlement. Wave after wave, day after day, until after six days he ceased. He had taken Lulu's body and wrapped it in the finest blanket she had brought from home, placed in it parfleches of meat and strung it outside, between two tall pines. And he had never left her, day or night, but hunched below for six days and nights, howled almost without stop. He then cut down her body, set it afire and watched until she was ashes. Three days later, after these had cooled, he gently scooped up some of the ashes with his hands and put what would fit into the quilled bag Lulu had brought with her on their trip home.

On the anniversary of her death, John has walked a pilgrimage from the cabin to the Settlement four times a year. When he returns home from each trip, his howls fill the air for six days. He loved his Pequot wife and he adored their child.

Damned if Herman didn't try tried to exterminate the whole race, to write them into extinction. "Pequod ... a celebrated tribe of Massachusetts Indians, now extinct as the ancient Medes." Hah—we refuse to die. And we aren't bastards.

Sophia

On one of my walks last week I saw someone who keeps coming into my field of vision, whether he is actually there or not. I do not know his name. I do not even know who he might be. But he was walking on the other side of Market Street and he was like nothing I had ever seen in the streets of Massachusetts. He was tall and very, very curved. He wore a blue-gray coat that cinched tightly at the waist and then flowed outward, terminating in folds cropped at knee-length. Knotted around his neck was a scarf—I imagine of silk—in a pattern of plaids of the deepest yellows, reds, greens and blues, one end—and one end only—of which was tucked into a vest of the purest white which topped trousers of blue and gray stripes, adding to the effect of the elegant length of his entire figure. The trousers did not completely end at his ankles however; I swear that a piece of them wound down around his boots and that he actually walked upon the end of his trousers! He was topped by an extraordinary hat that rose at least a foot from his forehead, with a brim as broad as his ample shoulders. The collar of his coat was rolled into a softly-sculpted fold and the front of his trousers closed with a row of buttons that shone with the luster of mother-of -pearl. At his waist was an elaborate fob, embroidered with what I am sure were gold seals, though I could not see the details. His hands were in what must have been side pockets cut and finished into the side seams of his trousers. Out of his right-hand pocket emerged what looked like a riding crop, though no steed was in evidence. The pointed end of this crop almost met the flowing, rippled, unsecured end of his scarf. From whence he came, I know not. When I turned back to get a view of his figure from the back, he had turned the corner and disappeared. But he returns to a corner of my mind where I can begin to feel the scarf fold about the riding crop, where I can feel his knotted breath in mine.

Lizzie

He compels me; Herman is the strangest, most magnetic man I have ever met. He has tattoos; I caught a glimpse of one under his shirt. He swears—a lot. He drinks, too. And he is always with other men. I have never seen him with any woman except me.

Sophia

Mother had so many children. Most of the women I know have had so many children. And our poor mother cat who died last year having given birth to yet another litter when she was old and frail. Her poor teats swelled so. No milk came forth, only the foul, thick, white poison that killed her. We tried to save all the kittens but could not, even though we all took turns getting up and trying to feed them every few hours. But one did survive. It's a calico, the only female of the litter. I do not know the significance of that if significance there is. We named the kitten Squeak because it has but the tiniest little voice a cat ever had. Unless you happen to see its mouth move, you would hardly hear its mew. But it is the sweetest little cat. It will curl into your lap for hours and its purr makes up for its lost voice.

Lizzie

Lulu and John's baby girl—Lulu Elizabeth Yellowbird Many Stars Hawkridge Hitchcock—grew to be a beautiful, honey-haired child with eyes a deep, true hazel. Her father told her many times her mother's favorite story about Yellowbird and Motley Dog. The child loved to hear the story, loved to imagine the rough smoothness of Yellowbird's cheek. When his daughter was seven, John made his last pilgrimage to the Settlement where he left her to be raised. After leaving their child, John set out on a journey from which he probably never returned. We know that he carried with him, hanging from a leather strap on his belt, the quill bag containing Lulu's ashes. Some say that he set out to find Yellowbird. The old-timers swore that John intended to ask Yellowbird to weave into her blanket Lulu's quills, quills now tinted with her ashes. He intended to unravel her bag, quill by quill, and watch the old woman make Lulu a part of the eternal world.

-Yellowbird-

Yellowbird recalls how it is that Blue Bottle Fly Girl lays her eggs in dead things. It was not always so.

In the First Time, Fly Girl and Fly Boy met and fell in love. He doted on her, made her feel safe and full and wonderful. Fly Girl loved to tell how he made love to her, how he brought so soft and gently his hairy legs to hers, how she could hear them vibrate before she could even feel his soft hairs join with hers. How they pricked her gently, making her shiver inside, ready and open to his probing.

Fly Girl was thrilled to discover she was pregnant. She sought out the most beautiful pond in the world, where her blue-black babies could nestle against the soft petals of a pink water lily. Blue and black and pink—oh how Fly Girl could imagine the translucent colors of her babies against the opaque pink. Their tiny wings would reveal many worlds and many things.

Fly Girl tells often how much she loved her little fly babies. Their little razor mouths sucking at her. A sweet, stinging, suck; her teats throbbed with pleasure. When the tiny hairs near their mouths brushed her nipples, Fly Girl felt at peace.

On the second day after their birth, Fly Girl left them to find food. Fly Boy had not brought any since the babies had been born. When she returned she discovered that Fly Boy had eaten the babies and torn apart the pink water lily. Strewn on the surface of the pond were pieces of pink and tiny shards of blue and black.

Fly Girl hated Fly Boy and yet still she desired him. She prayed to find some way to have him and to protect her next babies. She had a vision of dead, rotting meat; she knew it would be safe.

30

When her next babies were due, she left Fly Boy and found the most rotten carcass in the world. Her labor was terrible; her first babies had been born without pain. These babies came only after hours of agony, pain so sharp that her hind legs vibrated so loudly that their sound carried for miles. People came to say that when they heard the wind howl they knew that Fly Girl was in labor again.

When Fly Girl looked down at these babies she was horrified. They were white, wormy, nasty, maggoty things that had come out of her. No soft fur, no blue-black wings. But then she felt them, strangely soft, sticky-sleek, mouthing their way from her to the dead tissue upon which they had been born. They would feed there; they would leave her alone. In time, they would grow wings and they would keep the world clean. She was satisfied that all was as it had to be.

Sophia

I have been reading a good deal in Burns, Blake and Wordsworth. I find myself returning to a passage in her journal. I will write it here—I would like to feel the words take shape on the page. "As we were going along we were stopped at once, at the distance perhaps of fifty yards from our favorite birch tree. It was yielding to the gusty wind with all its tender twigs. The sun shone upon it, and it glanced in the wind like a flying sunshiny shower. It was a tree in shape, with stem and branches, but it was like a Spirit of water. The sun went in, and it resumed its purplish appearance, the twigs still yielding to the wind, but not so visibly to us. The other birch trees that were near it looked bright and cheerful, but it was a creature by its own self among them." Seeing the ink assume shapes on a page where there were none convinces me that words are a spirit waiting to be formed. And so I repeat this act with words from his poem. Not all of it, but parts.

> "There is a yew tree, pride of Lorton Vale,
> Which to this day stands single, in the midst
> Of its own darkness, as it stood of yore:
>
> Of vast circumference and gloom profound
> This solitary Tree! A living thing
> Produced too slowly ever to decay;
> Of form and aspect too magnificent
> To be destroyed.
>
> Huge trunks! And each particular trunk a growth
> Of intertwisted fibers serpentine
> Upcoiling, and inveterately convolved;
> Nor uniformed with Phantasy, and looks
> That threaten the profane;
>
> As in a natural temple
> United worship; or in mute repose
> To lie, and listen."

But I do not think this is sufficient. He didn't capture it. Perhaps a series of sketches, each separate and yet connected, which might begin with a female shape giving birth to a tooth-tongue of vast circumference and depth profound.

I have not been able to get ink of very good quality of late. It simply does not last as it should. Lately, before I can finish these entries, short as they are, the ink begins to pale so that I can hardly read the words that I have written and often find that I must use more so that I can go over and reform the words to make them legible on the page. But sometimes I just leave them very, very pale and wonder what I will read when I encounter them again. I have once or twice let the pen go dry and left just the quill-tipped shaped impression upon the page. This makes me wonder whether the words will exist if they do not have their inked shape visible.

Lizzie

"Herman has taken to writing poetry. You need not tell anyone, for you know how such things get round." — Lizzie Shaw Melville, to her mother

Sophia

As often as I can I walk abroad and visit the increasing number of shops that sell such wonderful curiosities. I cannot afford to buy one but I do—as often as I dare—go into the shop and examine a wonderful little jug painted with what is called the moss rose pattern. There is indeed an entire service painted with this pattern but it is the jug that intrigues me so. It really should be called a moss bud jug since none of the roses is even partly opened; all are in tight buds, knotted, as it were, against unfurling their sculpted petals. There is a hazy, hairy mossiness that covers each bud, almost as if it awoke from a slumber and pulled a carpet of moss over its tightly curled body. I have never seen such a rose and do not know whether it exists in nature or not. But they seem so real that I can almost feel the soft fuzz soften on the hard, cold, glazed clay.

It reminds me oddly of a watercolor mourning memorial that has hung in the front parlor at home ever since Catherine died. Mother's dearest friend did it to commemorate my sister's short, short life. It is a haunting scene, and not just because it depicts mother mourning at Catherine's grave. Mother is dressed in a black chemise, gathered under the bust and draping amply downward to her ankles. She wears a mourning bonnet—the top of which rises into a shape not unlike that of an urn—of white trimmed with black taffeta ribbon that ties in a bow under her right earlobe. Her left hand supports the end of a shawl in which she cradles her face. Her elbow rests upon the ledge of the lower half of the monument. The huge urn which is the top of the monument towers above her and the top of the urn almost disappears into a huge willow tree whose drooping branches frame both mother and the monument.

Both mother and the monument are shades of black and white. The huge, enveloping branches, done in shades of green tinted at times with whites and blacks, appear not so much like willow branches but rather like willow branches covered with moss ready to comfort and soften the hard angular bed on which mother rests. But this drooping moss is in the background only; not even one wisp of its fuzzy branch hands enters the foreground to touch mother. Further in the background is a church and house, but mother is alone at the grave. In the very foreground is a

35

bunch of lilies, ever the symbol of resurrection. But there is an opening in the ground that separates mother and Catherine from the lilies. And that opening—so narrow in its breadth but suggestive of an endless depth as the tufts of flowers growing on the lips of its open mouth appear to be disappearing into it, sliding out of my sight into the depths of the earth—separates me from all of them.

When I made Lizzie's wedding veil I didn't realize the significance of something I did. We chose together the starflower pattern, perfect I said for connecting the earthly and the heavenly passions intertwined in the upcoming event. It is a very, very intricate pattern that works only with the most delicate thread. Every inch took me an entire evening; I insisted on nothing short of perfection, a perfectly wrought, symmetrically balanced and ordered repeating pattern that swirled outward on either side from the central starflower that would cover her eyes. I worked it outward until the length was achieved and then I began to repeat it to achieve such depth that the veil would become one with the entire back of her gown. At some point during my making the latter part, I consciously altered the pattern. It was not a mistake and therefore I did not correct it. I never mentioned it either.

In his grief he named the baby girl Lulu Hawkridge Cock II. He had intended first to name her as he and Lulu had decided and then he intended to name her after her mother but when he wrote the name out on a piece of paper for the Settlement people he left off the Hitch. Not knowing any better, the Settlement people filed the paper at the government office.

Sophia

My landscape is finished but I am not satisfied. It is good—very good, in fact—and I am sure of my ability to judge art. It was the view I had from the western window of my studio room. I captured the depth of the hills in the distance; the color of the sky on a July evening near sunset; the daisies tired from the day's heat and the primrose's freshly opening night blooms. It was good but it was not right. I sat and stared and finally gave up. I could not understand what was wrong, why I should be so dissatisfied. I must have daydreamed for quite a while but suddenly I started. In the very center of a patch of those tired daisies, in the very center—the very black center of a daisy's heart—I brushed my stroke, texturing a depth that made me smell the fervid, spicy heat of midsummer. And I continued the outer edge of one of the strokes and touched it to one of the opening night blooms. This painting is done.

Lizzie

I have been having this terrible dream, over and over again. I have just given birth to my first child. When they bring it to me, I reach out, eager to bring it to my breast. I ignore the look of horror on their faces; I reach for what is mine. When I look down, I do not see the face of a human child. I see eyes, and teeth, and fur, like a halo or a mane, surrounding its head and covering its body.

I have no horror; it is mine. I bring it to my breast; it feeds. I swear it has been born with teeth. Damn it to hell, I say to myself, I love this thing, the way it pulls and bites and takes me into itself.

I wake, sad and empty because I have no beast-child at my breast.

Sophia

I try to set aside an hour at least in the late afternoon or early evening for reading poetry or stories or plays. I often like to read a passage and then revision it in my mind, fashioning it out in a sketch. Or, if I am reading Shakespeare, for example, I will try to envision anew one of the characters and figure how, if I were to create that character now, how I would dress him and how he might speak. I have had little success with Ophelia until now. I always thought of her as being dressed in white. I simply could not get this image of her out of my mind. But it came to me earlier today that we have been wrong about her all along. She should be dressed in luxurious fabrics—silks and crepes and velvets—layered into textures and vibrant with deeply-dyed colors. When she is drowned, the water will become a pool that reflects the depthed color of her tortured soul. I am not sure depthed is a word but it is what I mean. That would make her a living thing produced so vividly before our very eyes that she could never simply die.

I tremble as I put pen to paper but hope seeing the forms take shape before me, in the light, in ink that I can see comes from my pen, dark threads that come from my hand, will make them stop. Every time I close my eyes they start. But the bodkin is the worst, that needled hairpiece, that needle with eyes so large that you can run your tape through the laced hem. But it is lacing through me, right into the center of my eyes and drawing a tape that is coming from somewhere deep inside of me and drawing it right through my eyeball and sewing together my lids and then running up into the center part of my hair and stabbing into the cleft of my head and then back again to the other eye and sewing it closed tight. The thread keeps coming out of me, spun out of my mouth opened wide, a yawning gulf spouting endless yards of this filament thread, so thin I can barely see it but so strong that it lacerates and needles into me effortlessly. Just before my second eye is sewn shut, I realize that I can see no hand holding the bodkin.

Lizzie

I tell Pecker that she is the best damned storyteller ever. I love to hear her tell about Buster and his ghosts. Buster said he slept well and was warm most winter nights except when they got mad and snatched his blankets. They got cantankerous sometimes, just like people. That didn't bother Buster much, not so long as they were still doing things he could see. The time to worry is when they'd stop. He warned, "'Cause then they'd come inside you and take your vitals, just like they did to Ruth." Buster wasn't afraid, mind you; just wary. Sure he spent a few nights cold, but glad the ghosts were with the blankets.

Once in a while, though, they'd get downright ornery, like the time they threw hatchets at him. Right after he and Ruth set up housekeeping. He and Ruth had just lain down. The doors started flying open and the walls rattled and then they smelled something like old shoe leather and then the hatchets started flying around the room, one into the wall, another into the dresser. Then one landed between them, in the middle of the head of the bed. This one wasn't a hatchet. It was a tomahawk. Said it must have been like being in King Phillips' War. But it wasn't often they got as bad as that. Every once in while, though, they had to let off steam, just like people.

Sophia

I am almost ashamed of this but want to make a note of it, now that this first impression has passed. When we arrived in Havana I was assaulted by the noise everywhere. It was as if the pain in my head had been externalized in the city's sound and I was literally surrounded by it. I am not so sure that hell is hot as I had imagined it to be. It is just as likely that it is noise: incessant, violent noise. Parrots and macaws screaming everywhere; bells that ring all day and all night; vendors of every shape and description howling in a language yet foreign to my ears; gangs of children roaming and yelling; and yet more birds in appearance fantastical and in sound demonic. I was sure that we had descended into an as yet unrecorded circle of Dante's hell.

But how silly of me. I love Cuba and its people now. Don Fernando laughs and jokes and touches so freely and effortlessly. It has made me realize how little I have been around people who seem genuinely to enjoy living. He indulges me and has begun sitting for his portrait. It will not be easy; his complexity is knit into the uneven contour of his brow and the varied hues of his cheek. His face is an odd mixture of hard angles and soft curves; his jet-black hair which is actually almost blue-black is both curly and straight; and his eyes contain a depth that almost threatens to drown anyone who looks too hard into them. Those eyes—gentle pools and yet eddying waters at the same time. And how am I going to capture that mouth? I caught a glimpse of him the other day when his mouth was set somewhere in between a smile and a grimace, being, for that moment, neither one nor the other. If I capture it, can we bear to look upon it? It frightens me and I want not to think about it. And yet it excites me deeply.

Guajamon, Guajamon, Guajamon. I think I'll think of him as a genie who I can call forth by chanting his name. Don Fernando gave me this horse, assuming that I didn't know how to ride well and would want his most accommodating steed. I mounted; I wore no bonnet. I looked at Don Fernando and instantly he knew I wanted to ride. He gave me his whip; he fastened one of his spurs to my heel; I cracked and jolted and chanted. I felt the muscular contractions underneath me, between me, through me as the wind chilled the nape of my neck and the rush of wind opened my nostrils so that I could smell the very foam of his mouth. The circular curls along either side of my center part gave way, unloosed and falling, till all shoulder length of my mane flew straight out in back of me in vertical line and I shook and tossed my head, waving my hair in an arc behind and beside me. I straddled full apart, filled with magnetic power surging through my spurred heel.

Guajamon, Guajamon, Guajamon. The name is like a prayer. I fear that I am lost. But I am not unwell. I have never felt better in my life.

Lizzie

The midwife said that Lulu was probably dead within the hour after John set out. Lulu's womb must have ruptured in two, the way she bled so. It was bad, at first; her face all grimaced and twisted into knots. The more the baby screamed, though, the stiller Lulu got, so that before long her face wasn't twisted anymore.

Right at the end she spoke. She said "They're here. They're really here!"

Lulu had always said that the old timers swore that the animals would be there when you started your final journey. The eagle, the bear, the deer, the hummingbird—all of them—would walk you past the threshold of this life.

Sophia

It has been the fashion for some time in New England for us to fashion large, elaborately decorated hats. The one I was most proud of was the one I called my harvest hat. I labored for weeks to achieve the effect that would create the illusion that I was an animated cornucopia, spewing forth bounty as I walked abroad. It was an elaborate display of fruits and seeds and berries and nuts, all intertwined and connected through an elaborate network of interwoven ivy. I thought at the time, that I had indeed brought to fruition here an image of my true self. But I fear that I have been sadly mistaken, that I have harvested but an illusion. I know that I must weave with threads that are pulled not from the garden but from the center of my soul. But I do not know how to grasp them and pull them through.

Lizzie

I like it better with myself than I do with him. He is so hard. It stabs so. I am always grateful it is done. But I don't dare say no. He just might kill me.

But when it is just me, it is soft and gentle and I am sad when it is done, anxious to have moments—no, hours—alone to do it again.

Sophia

We left the Morrells' this morning and stopped to rest at Don Fernando's sister's house during the heat of the day. I have never seen such sensual, rich, frescoed walls. I have never seen such expanses of marble, softened by doorways curtained with a delicate, gauzy material. I have never seen such an array of rich tapestries, hung from nearly every wall, at least six feet in diameter and easily twice as high. Huge iron candelabra lighted the perimeter of the entry. The room was so cool, despite the intense heat just beyond the door. As you entered, it is as if you were sealed against the uncomfortable world. All the male family members bowed to us. On the domed and arched ceiling were armorial crests and winged angels, painted in a richness of color so deep, so resonant, that they gave the ceiling a pulsing depth. And oh the fragrance—no, the odor, the smell—that embraced us. By no means unpleasant—quite the contrary. It was a fervid, spicy, deep smell, exotic and yet common at the same time.

A Negro maid appeared and led us down one of the long, arched hallways. Lining the aisles were portrait upon portrait, ancestral portraits I assume. But how unlike a New England hallway in which hangs family portraits. The faces I met in those Cuban hallways were laughing, smiling, caught in a movement of some sort. Getting on a horse, in the middle of a dance, in an embrace. And the clothes. Bright, rich colors; deeply folded and embellished fabric. Silks and velvets. I became aware that the smell deepened and realized that we were led into a marbled bath. My sister Mary and I disrobed and were helped to enter a water so warm and fragrant that I felt it must have been like this to enter Elysium. I waved my hands around me under the surface of the water, creating little jets, little ripples that washed over me. I felt my nipples tighten as I ran my watered fingers over my breasts. I felt, . . . well, I felt Mary watching me. We left the water and were rubbed all over with a powder so fine and so deliciously fragrant that I cannot ever recall even reading about something so rare. And then we were slipped into robes of linen so fine that my hand coursed over it without feeling a harsh thread. Mary dressed and went back to the family. I, however, retired, to avoid a headache.

I was led to a huge bed, whose head was fully ten feet high, and canopied all around with linen as fine as the robe I wore. I slipped out of the robe, parted the linen veil, slid onto a coverlet of the finest silk I had ever touched. I lay back, moving my arms up and down at my sides, feeling the silk ripple, tense and then soften with each successive stroke. I fanned my hair out all around me and shook it from side to side, feeling it whip around me, giving full sway to the smell, opening mouth and eyes and legs, parting the center, the silken center of the dark light.

The next morning my hostess took me to her bedroom and showed me Murillo's Magdelan. Little could be seen of her; smoky grime had all but obscured her face. I noticed some aromatic oil on the table. I dipped my finger and touched a corner of the painting, swirling my tip in ever-widening circles. A deep crimson tint appeared. I continued until the entire painting was cleaned. She had glowing, golden hair that fell in waves around her head. She had large, deep, sad, deep-brown eyes. They said that I had worked a miracle as they saw the full revelation of her sorrowful, sorry face for the first time. They wanted me to take her back to America and copy her but I refused.

I really was not honest. The non-Indian man great-grandmother married was part Black. He was English and French Canadian and part Black, too. I don't know how much—it couldn't have been very much because he looked white—but he was part Black and in some states that makes him Black. Mother never would talk about it and I never dared ask father about any of it. In fact, mother got to saying that the story about John and Lulu was just all made up anyway. Not a lick of truth to any of it. That father—Chief Justice of the State no less—never knew anything about it because it wasn't true.

Herman tried to drown that part but couldn't. It rose—crazy, yes, but alive to a wondrous depth. Damn it Pip, your forty-dollar black soul is in mine and we will wander forever in the wilderness.

Sophia

We have bought an old, roomy house on Charter Street with a large front parlor for father's office. My headaches are so much better than they have been in years. They come much less frequently and last much less long. There is an old, overgrown garden in back that I have worked in for months and have recovered many of the stands of old perennials. In back of that old garden is an old burial ground. I have spent some time there, too. I have planted a special flower on the grave of a little girl. At her head, her parents have placed a stone lamb. At her feet, I have placed a fleshy, uncommon bloom. Mary brought some flower seeds from Cuba. I planted them in plain pots and tended them all winter; now they are set out in the summer garden. It really is wonderfully invigorating to be able to smell Cuba in this New England back yard. All the neighbors are curious about the plants but are not unanimous in their approval. The head of the local flower club said the petals were too thick, the colors too deep, the smell too overpowering and ruined the effect of the entire garden. But I think that they are the garden. I am going to paint it soon—just as soon as the large flame-orange orchid begins to set seed.

Lizzie

There was a blue bottle fly in the bedroom last night. Its buzzing nearly drove him into a rage. He threw his shoe, books, bolted from bed with the swatter in hand and hurled himself after it, only to miss again and again. With each miss, he raged louder, hurling curses, screaming at me, finally ripping the covers from the bed. He let go the swatter, sat at the edge of the bed, and sobbed.

"Lizzeee, I can't stand it. I can't even get the damned fly," he moaned.

The fly buzzed about his head, then followed the ceiling around the perimeter of the room, only to return and buzz right over the top of his head.

"You damned blue black sonofabitch," he yells, standing up, swatter back in hand. "I'll kill you if it's the last thing I do," he vows.

I return to bed, reclaim the covers and shield myself from the weight of him landing on the bed and then jumping from it, and then landing on it again in an endless chase around the perimeter of the room.

In the morning neither he nor the fly was in the room. I prayed the fly escaped.

Sophia

I find that I am also returning in my mind to Emily, finding her way through the mazes of those long, dark, portraitured hallways in Udolpho. My mind's eye recalls the very words as I encountered them on the page. Annette's warning that Emily risked losing herself further if she continued. But Emily continued through the long passages, until one opened into a suite of tapestried and ancient chambers, pervaded by a coldness that even the heavy, textured fabrics could not warm. And then her feeble light chanced upon the picture covered with the veil of black silk. She vowed to return later, when daylight had reanimated her spirits, and examine the picture at length. And return she indeed would, fascinated and terrified by the mystery of the veil and Annette's repeated warnings. I remember almost verbatim this passage: "A terror of this nature, as it occupies and expands the mind, and elevates it to high expectation, is purely sublime, and leads us, by a kind of fascination, to seek even the object from which we appear to shrink." So Emily was led onward, through the corridor-maze of those long, sinuous hallways. Led to the dark part of the room, to the heavily framed veil that she lifted. And then she let it fall, concealing from her sight the picture that she now knew was no picture. If this were my novel, I would know that when she lifted that black veil, she saw herself. Mouth open, ready to speak, stepping forth from the frame. If she had not let it fall again, she could have threaded herself out of the maze. But, alas, her timid hand lets go.

Lizzie

He was at the door, violets in hand. I did not say the right thing, as always. Herman crushed the violets, lurched past me, into the house, locking the door behind him. "You bore me," he muttered, when he was safely out of my reach.

Sophia

I received a package from Cuba. The Morrells sent it to thank me for so miraculously cleaning the Magdalen. Actually it isn't from Cuba, exactly. Mrs. Morell was in Europe and bought there the most exquisite fabric imaginable. It is a blue that flies off from your eyes when you gaze upon it. I swear, it is the very color of the bluebird in flight. Not the bluebird at rest, mind you. But the bird, blue wings open, through which light filters into little shards that gather the reflection of the world. I have never felt fabric like this before. It is silk but silk that is quilted throughout with a variety of patterned stitches, creating a palette of shapes, as it were. But I am not accurate when I say it is a blue. It is really two blues that have melted together to create a single blue that moves with the fluid power of twinness. If you look closely, you can see that the fabric is really softly striped. And it is wonderfully fitting that the stripes are not broken by the quilting stitches. No—if anything, they ripple for a moment and then continue their own movement as if they had not been interrupted at all.

Lizzie

Before he brought her to the Settlement, John Hawkridge Hitchcock told his daughter what her full name ought to have been. Lulu Elizabeth Yellowbird Many Stars Hawkridge Hitchcock. She laughed, a laugh as soft as grass and deep as seas. Lizzie Cock'll do me just fine, she said as she pursed her lips to say it once and then opened wide to say it a second time.

When I am feeling just so, I imagine that she says Cock-a-doodle-do, any cock'll do.

Sophia

I can hardly wait to begin. I am going to make my own version of the pelisse. I am going to make the dress and then I am going to make the cloak more like a man's vest. It will be sleeveless and just fit over the bodice of the dress. I will taper it on each side so that when it falls across my bosom the upper part will touch the very center of my breast and then fall away, cupping its increasingly narrow self toward my arm. It will be stiff enough, however, to hold its own shape and will stand out from my body, floating in the air at about the juncture of the inside of my elbows. The vest will have a rounded collar, not at all close to the neck, and be gathered loosely with a bow made from the ends of the collar. The dress will have sleeves that gather softly at the shoulder, then fall along the natural curve of my arm. I am tempted to have the cuffs extend below my hands. The dress will be of little form, save that which comes from tying a wide sash around my middle. The weight of the fabric alone will ensure enough of a drape to the floor to balance the width of the shoulders. The dress itself will be free from any other ornament; the fabric is itself rich and textured sufficiently. The way that I will fashion the vest will give the illusion that I am in flight, winging past you, cutting the light into prisms that reflect a world gathered under the long weight of the dress.

I will have fun, I think, working on this during our weekly sewing circles. Often I will try to work alone on such projects. But I think that I will take delight in beginning this one in public. And I am so looking forward to going to Cornelia's next week. Lizzie and I are going up; Cornelia has invited us to what is billed as the affair of the decade. She has promised us that we are to meet with every radical thinker on this side of the Atlantic—and a few that she has imported for the occasion.

I am getting really uneasy about Sophia—she pretends that she is free but she is not. I have seen her with him. He is more gentle than mine, but he has snared her just the same.

"Oh, Lizzie, I think that I will not be able to go to Boston next week," she cried.

"Why not," I protested, "the trip has been planned for weeks."

"Well, when I mentioned it to Mr. Hawthorne, he sighed that he had hoped to spend that day with me."

"Well, can't he spend another day with you? Why does it have to be that day? Does he own your time?" I cried.

"No, but I think it best anyway to do as he suggests," she said, with an emphasis on he.

But I know it is more than a suggestion. He has got her.

-Yellowbird-

First Mother told Yellowbird about how to gain protection from any man on earth by burying his hair. First Mother protected herself from First Father by cutting a piece of his hair, wrapping it in rawhide, tucking it into a quilled case, and burying it deep in a wood, a wood so deep that no one would be able to find it. She walked very, very softly deep into the wood so the impression she left with her foot would be nearly invisible.

First Mother said that from that time forth all her earth daughters would never have to worry about being abandoned or abused. If evil things started, all First Mother had to do was walk back to that deep wood, unbury the hair, hold it in her hand, and knot it in her fingers. Once knotted tight, she would pull it taut through her teeth and bite, bite hard. As she did so, he would fall, weakened and feeble, unable to stand against her.

Yellowbird laughed when she saw Lizzie take his hair, wrap it in oil-cloth, place it in a beaded bag, and bury it in back of their Arrowhead house, in the field at the base of the Berkshire Mountains. She chuckled, too, when she saw their dog dig it up a week later. In the old times, she told herself, there might have been woods deep enough to keep the burial site secret. But for the new times, we have to adjust things. Yellowbird and Motley Dog knew that Lizzie's safety had nothing to do with his hair, buried or unburied. They had faith that one day Lizzie would walk the earth without fear.

Yellowbird knew that Lizzie would learn to make something with her hands, something so fine that she could walk into the deepest of woods or the freshest of fields leaving hardly a trace of her coming. Motley Dog nodded, noticing Lizzie take the bundle from the dog's mouth, laugh, and throw it all away.

58

Sophia

Father's assistant, Dr. Fiske, began my treatments a week ago. He has had great success with his mesmerism, though his is of a different sort than the others in town. He and father have performed perfectly painless tooth extractions by mesmerizing the patient. Those who have undergone the treatment bear testimony to its effectiveness. But it has not increased their business as much as they had hoped. At first, I felt calmed, soothed almost, by the treatments. He would suspend a shape and I would concentrate on it, watching it pulse and concentrating harder and bringing together my eyes so that finally it stopped moving altogether and I had the sensation of being suspended in time. I was very aware of everything around me; I could hear the clock tick and chime but it was if I was not hearing the sounds. They were being heard but I was not doing the hearing. He would tell me that my headaches would be gone and I would repeat; he would say that I would be able to sleep and I would repeat. I was wide awake and very conscious that I was parroting him and yet I could swear that I had not said a word. And then he would tell me that the session was going to end and then it would be over. It all sounds perfectly ridiculous and yet I felt a calm, a feeling of wellness that I cannot deny. But a few hours later the pain returned, incessantly.

So he was going to use the very depth of mesmerism, as he called it, during which I would no longer be awake, where I would achieve a level of being that would allow him to fuse his thoughts with mine. It was not enough in my case that I repeat his words; I had to live his thought, to feel the truth of his words so deeply that they became the thoughts in my own mind. But he could not. He tried and tried but I saw and heard the very breath of him take shape before me and push itself ever closer to my mouth, to the lips parted in uttering the words that he moved closer with until finally he was the word made shape suspended before me and pulsing into me. I had felt a sigh-breath sucking and shaping itself into me before. His form lengthened into a stiletto, a wide-eyed stiletto that began stabbing my eyes. I closed my mind and my heart to the shape of its sound.

I begin to despair that there is no hope for me.

Lizzie

Godey's, Godey's Godey's. I am sick of these pages filled with women in such stupid dresses. I like a trim waist—but I like to breathe too. And the hats—good lord, they are so big they make even a stout woman seem a dwarf. And the weight! I tell you, when my hay fever is bad, the sheer thought of one of them on my head makes the ache so profound that I scarcely believe I'll survive. That old woman Lulu talked about who wore rawhide. Now that's something that's practical, at least. I hate to sew; women always have to sew. But I will fashion something that fits, even if it kills me.

Sophia

I am troubled by my inability to make a connection among things that keep crowding into my mind. I think often about sewing and the very movement of the needle through the fabric. And I recall an old method of transporting contraband to the soldiers. Women would sew things into the folds of their heavy hems and deliver them on the field. There is significance, I know, in this image of the power of the hemmed border, a border hemmed by threads meant to be pulled loose. And then I think about spider webs and seeds. Why sewing and sowing are so different and yet so alike. And I am reminded then of Milton's reminder that the seeds will bruise the heel of Satan. And then Winthrop's warning that Anne Hutchinson would be delivered of a monstrous birth produced of several lumps of man's seed without anything from her in it. There are many days like this where I am crowded with thoughts like this that I know, somehow, are connected. But I cannot see the thread that joins them.

But I do marvel at the sheer strength of thread. I was helping mother change the sheets; we change the bottom one every two weeks but the top one only once a month. She embroidered these long before her marriage and they are still sound. The small tears that have occurred she has been able to repair easily. As I stood there, covering the bottom sheet with its unwashed top and then putting the pillows into their cases, I was struck by the delicacy of the handwork that has proved so durably strong. To realize the sheer smallness of each stitch is to marvel that mother has eyes left to see much of anything with. The threads, alas, have yellowed, but they have held tight, still strong enough to keep the seams from being torn asunder, still strong enough to hold the shape of their pattern. I imagine her, younger than I am now, fingering silken threads through her hands, pulling minute loops through front and back, building ever so slowly a mound of thread that rises ever so slowly from the face of the fabric.

I wonder if she would have taken such care had she been able to see what has been born under those linens.

I find that I am increasingly unwilling to spend much time embroidering my aprons as I am supposed to do. I cannot understand why I should spend so much time and energy on something which becomes so soiled and torn after such little use. Even when they are made of the strongest materials and the stoutest of stitches. If you have never beaten a rug, you will not understand what I mean. But if you have, you will have no trouble feeling the enveloping grit and grime tear into each tiny little stitch.

Lizzie

I am still bothered by his tattoo. Not the rose on his arm but the other one. It excited me before I saw all of it. It took some time before I saw him undressed with his back toward me. Now it really worries me. Why would a man want to have a cock incised on his spine? It crows every time he sits.

Sophia

I will never forget my first look at him; he was standing in the front hallway just as I turned to descend the last course of the stairs. I had not been holding the rail, wanting to appear perfectly centered and carelessly descending. I stopped, fixed to the spot, and held on for dear life. If I had not gripped with force enough to whiten my hand I swear I would have tumbled headlong. This lasted but a fraction of a moment. He saw me—he looked up first but then he fixed his gaze and saw me, not through me or around me but saw me—and I let go, perfectly centered and balanced and finished my descent effortlessly and eagerly. To be honest, I finished my descent fervently eager. Those blue-black eyes at the bottom unhatted me, put me on that Cuban horse, radiated shape into shape and galloped to the clouds, now gathering ever more strong and potent in the East.

The next week he came again. I wore pearls, the ones my sister Elizabeth had given me. Last week I wore a simple white linen dress. This week I topped a similar one with a shawl made of royal blue silk that I had embroidered with orange flowers. We sat in the parlor where he read to us from some of his most recent work. I showed him some of my most recent as well. Briefly, from time to time, we would be left alone. It was time enough. I have been magnetized to my very core.

This morning he came again but this time we escaped the house. We have been together the entire day and I have never felt better in my life. There has not been even the hint of a headache. We went to the woods where we roamed till the late afternoon, walking and talking, and singing and laughing with an abandon that I scarce realized possible. I wore the blue shawl again but this time over a yellow linen blouse and emerald woolen skirt. Mary had stared in horror at me; so did mother who didn't say a word. I know she disapproved or at least a part of her did. But I imagined that a part of her did not. My hat completed things. It had multi-colored plumes that extended the frame of my head upward and outward; I was the embodied representation of a Cuban parrot come to life in Salem! He would soon understand, however, that I was no parrot. I would speak with a voice that came from within me. I made a point of touching the pearls at my neck with some frequency.

We stopped in a small meadow. I was not shy. I told him that I had tried to draw him but could not get his image to my satisfaction. I could not get the proper light on his hair, could not manage the contrast between hair and skin. And I could not begin to capture the fullness, the complexity of mouth or eyes. I asked him if that had happened to him with his characters. If he had he ever tried to write someone's description and failed. He said that it happened when he really didn't know enough about the character he was trying to draw. That he would have to stop, try to imagine that character from its inside out, what he or she would see or feel or do, and then try the words again. When he knew enough, the words would work. But not before. Ah, I said, I can imagine that working for a character. But I am not trying to capture a character. Ah, then, he said, you will have to try another method. I returned that I had thought so. However, like our professions, they required that we listen to different voices—or perhaps listen to the same voices and yet hear different things.

I can scarcely wait till tomorrow. He is coming again in the morning and we will walk again. I know exactly what I must know before I can draw him to my satisfaction. It is not enough that I embody an idea of him. I want to embody him. I plan to return us to the meadow tomorrow.

We have returned to the meadow often. I have finished my portrait of him and we are both satisfied.

Lizzie

I don't like the look in his eye. He pierces right through me. Hawthorne wants me, I know it. I tried to talk myself out of it but I can't. Why else is it that he keeps finding some excuse to come by? Why else is it when I start to talk about Sophia he changes the subject? There's something dark and brooding and frightful about him that excites me. There's a violence, a passion, I am sure, underneath that gentleman's outfit. And I wouldn't be surprised to find a tattoo under that neat frock.

Sophia

This fall has been one of the longest and warmest that I can remember. The melon-orange hues of the fields set off against the clear of the sky; the softness of the sun upon your cheek and the crisp of leaves crunched beneath your feet; the ever waning daylight rekindled in the fire in the parlor at evening. I have taken such delight in walking into the woods and finding the very last blooms of the season. Almost as an afterthought, nature sets forth a single daisy in the field, its little yellow eye bravely storing as much daylight as it can. There is a fragrance to the air now that I find that I prefer to that of spring. This air has depth; it makes your lungs swell to full capacity as you drink it in. I do not agree with all the poets who say that spring is the season for love. It is rather the fall, I think, because its fragrance grows from the life that has been and not just the life that might be.

Lizzie

The day started well enough though I was left, as usual, to pass time with Sophia while Herman and Hawthorne went off into the hills. Sophia really is a dear but she is so very guarded. I can't quite ever be myself with her. She'd die if I ever told her how I really feel about things. I once tried—to tell her just how things were, I mean. I had merely started—"Sophia, it's so damned awful"—when she took my arm, pressed it hard—very hard, in fact,—and said, simply, with a firmness that bordered on hardness: "No. I will not hear this. Not today. Not ever. Not ever again." So we talk of dishes, sewing, clothes, food and even of these things we say little. Yet these outings are rather pleasant, after all, and I do so enjoy the fields at the bottoms of the hills, filled even with talk of only small things.

They returned for lunch—oh and what a fine lunch it was that we made. Chicken, fresh peas, strawberries, bread and cake—a rich, egg custard cake. Well, normally they would have sat and eaten with all the jovial energy a good talk in these hills ever engenders. But Hawthorne showed little appetite, his eyes turned toward the hills, as if he wanted to take back something he had found there. I felt the pall. I don't know if Sophia did and, even if she did, she probably would show no sign. I know that all is not right. His eye, small as it is, gets such a dark depth that I fear I will fall into it and drown.

Sophia

I have been reading my sparse entries for this year and am ashamed that I have not written more. But there are times lately when I do not want to commit my thoughts to paper. I do not want to give them such solid form. Perhaps if I do not shape them in ink, they will cease to be. I do not know what is wrong with me. I am happier than I think I have ever been. I am turning out paintings at a fast pace and have been selling them almost as quickly. I have had virtually no headaches for the longest time now. And I am falling so deeply in love that it thrills me right through the sole of my embroidered slipper in which I am wiggling my cold toes as I write this. And yet a dark cloud shapes itself in the back of my brain and I have begun to be afraid to look into the reflecting glass. I would pray that it goes away but I find that I am not a woman of that kind of faith.

Mother seems to be resigned to the idea that I am interested in marriage. I have always thought that she indeed must be so worn after bearing so many children and that is why she fears marriage so. But I do not intend to have even half as many. And I do not intend to become half so worn as she.

Lizzie

I am almost grateful that Herman leaves so often. If I make him stay he broods so. And then he talks about me in the third person, as if I wasn't here. Incompetent. Ugly. Damned crazy. Dull. Squaw. I am grateful that he goes so often abroad. Herman, a fine name for him. Her or man, which is it?

Sophia

I have seen an advertisement for a stove that has positively intrigued me. It is rather difficult to describe but I will try. The bottom half, though certainly striking and well done, is not very extraordinary. Rising from bracketed feet is the dome-shaped firebox atop which sets an urn—embellished with elaborate lion-head handles and a lion-shaped figure atop its cover—to hold the supply of coal. But what fascinates me is what grows from the back of the firebox, rises, and grows into an arch over the urn. There are two tree trunks which emerge from the base at the back of the dome; the handles of the urn join with them, creating the sense that the coal supply somehow feeds into the trunk—or I can fancy that the coal does indeed feed this iron trunk. It is at this juncture that the leaves begin and the trunks start to bend inward and to grow branches from which grow a thick canopy of leaves. The inward-bending branches and the thick veil of leaves meet in a point, creating the illusion that the lion is resting in a bower. The detail of these figures and the smoke pipes disguised as trees is exquisite, especially when you consider the material from which this is wrought. Imagine what warmth radiates from its stiff iron form. Imagine what wooly warmth relieves the stiffness of its iron joints. Never, I think, has a bower been more rigidly artificial and yet never, I think, have I been so persuaded of its ability to warm and sooth both body and soul. And never before have I felt that black could color a piece so effectively.

Lizzie

I had him. Down by the pier, hearing the horns pierce the distant fog. The moon wasn't full; it was but a sliver in the dark, overcast sky. Few stars were visible. The sand scratched like bits of glass and stuck to my back and sides. It hurt. It was over quickly. I told him I wanted to walk home alone. Hawthorne cried. There was no tattoo, after all. He was blank, white, unwritten.

Sophia

We would gather around a very large yet rather shallow, circular crock that was filled with a murky liquid of little smell and deep blue hue. Each of us would hold one end of an iron rod; the other end floated underneath the water line, assuming the variously distorted shapes common when we view underwater forms. The use of this liquid, I understand, is very symbolic as well. Mesmer believed that all things—celestial, terrestrial, and animated beings—are united and vivified by a universal fluid. Often, a good deal of time would pass before someone would have the first reaction—or the healing crisis as he called it. Someone would cry out, laugh, shake or sing, thereby releasing the flow of magnetic life force that united us all in the fluid freedom of its healing force. As often as not, it was the mesmerist himself who had this first crisis. And as often as not, we would let go of the iron rod, sit and converse still in the circle and then begin to wander without it, through the halls and other parlors, sampling an array of delicacies arranged on small tables and on the large sideboard in the central dining room. This room was connected to all the other rooms on the floor by a series of halls and pass-throughs. As often as not, there would be no individual sessions and the evening would end after our repast.

Whether it had been there before I cannot say but I remember that this was the first time that I noticed it. I wandered from the dining room to the end of the furthest hallway which seemed to conclude in a hinged screen painted with an Egyptian landscape. I went to examine the landscape but discovered a portrait hung behind it. This portrait arrested me, charmed me to the spot. Just as I began to examine it, I was called back, Lizzie having shouted that it was time to leave. I vowed then and there to return to it as often as I might so that I might begin to unveil its oddness, its powerful, unexpected otherness. I thought, with a thrill and a laugh, of Emily at Udolpho. Even if I had thought for a moment that I was, that I am not the heroine of a gothic romance was brought home to me in a flash. I happened to bring my right hand to my brow in order to brush off a fly. I noticed that my palm bore the imprint of the iron rod, apparently having been slightly rusted from its contact with the water. This reddish residue brushed off easily, however.

I think of this often and feel—as I have felt before and with increasing conviction—that there is a connection, a thread among all of these things that escapes me. As I write this, something suggests itself to me: Blake's illuminated, mystic painting. I have never seen it but I have read a detailed description and can feel the power even second-hand. That muscular figure whose forearm ripples with tensed strength and whose fingers bifurcate along held lines of an electric, magnetized compass that forms an inverted V. Blake said that he did not need the visible world; he painted only from his visions of the invisible. But I know that I need the visible world if I ever hope to get a glimpse of the invisible.

Lizzie

Herman's writing has gone very well and I swear he is not the same man as he so often is. He is calm, loving almost, and does not speak about me. At times I swear he actually seems to like me, to want to be with me. I think he almost thinks I am not ugly. Not dull. He said I was looking well. But I cannot grasp too hard this other self. I know too well that it is chameleon and fleeting. But, oh, I am so damned tempted! When he transforms, so do I.

Sophia

I can hardly describe the expansion of myself that I feel during and after the conversations that I have begun to attend with Elizabeth and Lizzie. Margaret is always the leader but she does not lecture. She leads us into a topic that starts the conversation of the evening, though often we end up conversing about something much different. She is a large woman and she is dressed gorgeously, but I find that when she begins to speak that I do not see her confined within the outlines of her body. It is as if she begins to push them outward, pulsing and growing with each parting of her lips. I know this sounds most odd, indeed, but it is the way it seems to be. Ben Jonson may have been right about men when he wrote that "No glass renders a man's form or likeness so true as his speech." But I do not think that this is true for a woman—or at least for a woman like Margaret Fuller. It is her very speech that makes me realize that her real self is so much more than her form or likeness—and I do not just mean her physical frame. What I mean is that her language reflects but a portion of what I believe is the entirety of her unframed soul.

And yet she is not happy, despite her enormous talent and accomplishment. She wrote to Elizabeth that "I have known some happy hours, but they all lead to sorrow, and not only the cups of wine but of milk seemed drugged for me." I felt so lonely for her when Elizabeth read this to me and I feel even more lonely as I have now re-recorded them upon my page. What strikes me is the odd correspondence she draws between wine and milk. Whether she envisions herself at the communion altar or at her mother's breast, it seems neither man nor woman nor deity can relieve her pain. I would pray for her if it was prayers that I thought she needed.

I have had an odd daydream recur to me of myself painting a canvas filled with hair. The hair is full, wavy, dark; the play of light upon it creates the sensation in the viewer of having hands upon the hair, feeling the waves and the fullness ripple darkly through your fingers. There is only hair. There is no face whatsoever, not even the hint of one.

He said that Benjamin Franklin himself said that indeed all the Pequot were killed in King Phillips' War and that Chandler's History records their extermination.

"Such lies," I retorted. "I don't have to believe it," I insisted.

"What the hell do you know about it anyway? Do you know a live Pequot?" he taunted. "Don't tell me you had dinner with one of them" he snarled.

"And a fine one we had," I shot back, getting out of his way quickly.

Sophia

After the weekly conversation ended an incident with Connie has been in my mind ever since. We kept our seats in front of the carved leaf door, with its garland made whole by its pieces being released from the dark recess into which they were usually parted and pushed. Connie shifted her chair, though, so that she faced the door and she put her hands on either side of my head, holding my head in direct alignment with her own. She looked into my eyes, commanding absolute silence and concentration. We were to hear each other breathe and to regulate our breaths to each other, to the breaths that were the same tempo and force of the beat of our hearts and which imaged its sound in the flickering lights of the pupils of our eyes which began to pulse and sparkle and shape themselves—first smaller and then larger, first dilating and then narrowing and then dilating again—to the rhythms of our hearts and our breaths. I cannot explain it but it was as if time disappeared, as if the doors behind me opened wide and ushered us into a room that I had not only never entered before but that I also did not even know was in the house. That room was carpeted in the thickest of Brussels wool and I walked upon it with feet bare. I felt the soft wool needle into the soles of my feet and felt my toes pattern themselves over the carpet, erasing the medallions that were there and recovering them, creating great leafy expanses, not of acanthus, but of fern, and not fern dried and pressed into paper shapes and hung on the wall in a frame like I had done before, but ferns swept into life that repeated and fanned outward from my toes for as far as my eyes could see. And I was sitting on an ottoman that must have been straight from the Turkish empire, upholstered in the richest of deep orange-red damask, tufted and fringed on all sides. I sat there and discovered that the fringe fingered itself up through my naked toes and wound itself through and around my now-completely-bare me and I felt the wind fan the fringe into my hair and out behind me and then back again to the nape of my neck. And then I was in time again, dressed, sitting upright in the chair, doors closed. I felt a calm, a religious calm that I have never felt before. It was then that I began to believe that I had discovered God behind those open doors.

Lizzie

He took his tongue to me. I wrapped my legs around his head and held his hair and came and came and came. And then I mounted him and rode and rode and rode. And then I took him in my mouth and I sucked him dry.

Sophia

I want to confess two things. First is that I had us move the dining room table into the front parlor; we have the audacity regularly to dine there—and very often. And so then I made the dining room my study. On the northern side, windows overlooking Concord Bridge. On the western, windows overlooking the back of the property, the gardens, the river and beyond to the mountains. His study was just above, with the same views, but the windows above were but half size. I need the light more than he. I said that I wanted to confess only two things but it is really closer to three. After supper that first night, we moved the dining room table. The perimeter of the room held a number of case pieces—a sideboard, a bonnet-top chest, a cupboard. But the center of the room was now the field of the thick, plush, figured carpet, repeating figures that fanned out from a central medallion and ended in a series of borders that contained smaller versions of the central medallion. Upstairs, in our bedroom, was the second-hand bed that I had painted with an allegorical motif on both headboard and footboard so that when we would stretch ourselves we could literally touch dawn and night anytime we wanted to. But we did not go there this night. We went instead to the dining studio. I disrobed and stood before him naked, save for the pearls at my neck. I was not shy. When we lay down, it was on a carpet medallioned with my meadowed self, and with both of us taking turns being astride.

Lizzie

I am learning to do quill embroidery. It will not be easy. And I must remember always to cut off the sharp tips. Otherwise they will penetrate you, will ensnare you.

But I will remember their barbed tips and I will take care. I will make a pair of moccasins so fine that even Lulu couldn't have imagined them.

Sophia

I well remember that even on my wedding day mother could not let go of her fear. Still, though, it was a fine day. After heavy rain all the day before and well into the early morning, the sun cleaved its way through a mist-filled dawn to create a clear and bright mid-morning. It was as if we were not on West Street at all, to look out and watch the fog lift its veil from the landscape it had so shrouded from our view. The wet light left clinging to the land gave a radiance to the earth that fills you with the faith that the hand that created this must have fingertips with an exquisite sense of touch.

There were few people in attendance, save my family, and closest friends. Elizabeth wanted to have a late afternoon or evening wedding so the whole of Boston and Concord and Salem could be in attendance. But my sister Mary, bless her, agreed with my desire for more privacy. The wedding was held in the morning and the back parlor, where we took our vows, was mercifully screened off from the former front parlor, now turned West Street Bookshop. Sarah, dear friend and fellow artist, braided my hair. Connie, whose friendship and patronage has meant so much to me, whose hands have opened me to what had been an unseen world, wound pond lilies—just gathered with the dew still upon them—around the braids that circled my head and swept themselves and the lilies into a delicious knot at the nape of my neck. I felt the power of her hands more than I had ever felt them before. It was as if the dew on the flowers that she had just picked chilled through me and released their warmth in the very center of my being. They sent an electric impulse throughout the whole of me. I was calmed and fortified as never before. And I was so aware of her generous nature. She was genuinely happy for me and is here with me, in spite of her own failed marriage and the impending divorce. He is wrong about her, so very wrong. She is not a dangerous influence upon me. She is my own best measure of myself. If it were not for her, I would have never known all the rooms in this house.

But just as I was descending the stairs, dressed in a richly simple gown of white satin with a tunic of matching fabric embroidered with white silk and wearing pearls at my neck, the clouds gathered quickly in the East. Just as I passed the curved landing in the stairs, the glass in the window that overlooks the pond was spattered with rain. I looked out for the last time as an unmarried woman through lenses stained and spotted and which made everything glow with the haze of dirty little halos. Reverend Clarke stood with his back to the doors of the closed-off front parlor. The garland of acanthus leaves carved atop the doors formed an odd and imposing background for the man. I turned to look at mother and have ever since regretted having done so. If I had not known better, I would have sworn that she was about to witness my conversion to Catholicism—or worse. All life seemed gone from her face. She seemed a ghost going through the motions of life. None of his family was in attendance.

I will confess something about which I must admit I am a bit ashamed. As Reverend Clarke was reading the vows to which we would assent, I began to hear voices come from within the front parlor, heard words form themselves into a garland that rested for a moment atop the acanthus one before removing from that spot and reforming itself into a chain of lilies that secured themselves around the nape of my neck. I felt the thrilling power of them tingle through me. I vowed that I would never forsake that feeling.

But the sun soon shone again and we left West Street to begin our marriage journey to Concord in a carriage that bounced me high into the air, as high or higher than I had ever been bounced before, even in Cuba.

Lizzie

The wedding was short and rushed.

"I do," he bellowed.

"I do," I gasped.

-Yellowbird-

Yellowbird and Motley Dog tell many stories to pass the time these thousand of years. Motley Dog loves to tell this one each summer, just as the corn tassels. There was a brave warrior, Spotted Hawk, who fell in love with a gorgeous woman from a tribe with whom his people had been at war. The elders forbade their union. Spotted Hawk and Lonely Flower fled together, bound by their love and desire.

In nine months, Lonely Flower gave birth to a strange creature. It was made up of all sorts of parts stuck together—female, male, buffalo, wolf, eagle, turtle, earth, water—around which was a long, shaggy mane. They loved this child-creature, held it, rocked it, sung to it and called it their strange and special one. Lonely Flower did her best to feed the strange one but her breasts, heavy with milk, found no relief. This strange and special child creature had no mouth with which to suck its mother's gift. So they gathered water and made soup and fed it through its many openings but whatever they put in just leaked out.

For four days they tried desperately to feed their offspring and prayed to the Great Spirit that delivered them this treasure to hear their plea. Lonely Flower offered the Great Spirit her milk in return for its life. But it died just the same. They mourned for many days and nights and then set out together once more, never to be seen again.

When they reappear Motley Dog knows that then the Great Spirits will renew the world, will make dogs the chosen ones, to stir the pots and weave the world again and again and again.

Sophia

I have a keen interest in something that Margaret is thinking about writing. We have talked often in our group about what America is and what kind of art it needs to produce. I sometimes have the feeling that they are not conscious of me as an artist, especially since so many of my scenes are often copies of European landscapes. But I have been listening intently and thinking intensively. Margaret has written down phrases that may appear in the finished essay and has shared them. She calls us a "mixed race continually enriched with new blood." And unless we can produce an art equal to capture and to reflect that vital intensity we will produce nothing but "abortions like the monster of Frankenstein, things with forms and the instincts of forms, but soulless and therefore revolting." There is a chilling truth to what she claims. I know that my husband is capable of producing such fully completed conceptions; I have faith that he will but fear that he may not. I also know that a copyist like me produces mere abortions, and nothing more, no matter how fine the line, how detailed the shadings. And I have caught glimpses of the soul that I wish to paint; I have had glimpses where I can envision myself brushing into life a being bloodied with vital intensity. I have faith and I have fear.

When I told Margaret of my engagement to him, she was very happy and excited. I hear her words now. "There is enough of the woman in him—and the man in you—to satisfy each other without obliterating each other." Oh, I must have faith in these words.

But he voiced a very unsettling judgment about women who write novels and other forms that are intended for a public audience. He said that they prostituted themselves and he was very glad that I did not. This has disturbed me and I brood over it. I do not think that women writers prostitute anything. And I am deeply disturbed by his choice of verb. I did not speak at the time. I need to think this through more carefully before I do. And I have never let on that I have been going—with Elizabeth and Margaret and all of us who still gather at the bookshop for our conversations—to the mesmerist over on Fulton Street, the one who advertises that he can help us unveil the powerful aura that is the source of our electric energy. I do not agree with my husband that a mesmerist can take your soul. I am not even convinced that a mesmerist has any power over you at all, that it's not a lot of fancy words and illusion. But I do know that going to the mesmerist is something I have done and will continue to do. I feel there is a force that comes from deep inside of me and I want to find out its details. And there is the portrait at the far end of the front parlor. It draws me. And so I will continue to go although I choose to be silent about it at present. I will not be silent always; I remember Ophelia.

Lizzie

Sophia keeps telling me how she can't figure out Ophelia. I don't say anything; it would be of no use. I know what happens to Ophelia. Women always drown.

Sophia

I have not been able to record this for some weeks but now I must. It was a bright, cold night, stars flashing the sky and earth, a clear, bright cold that reverberated into a thrilling metallic taste on one's tongue. The moon was nearly full; its light joined the light of the stars and swathed us in a shaft of wholeness that highlighted and illumined our shadowed figures as we edge-bladed our paths across the frozen river, swirling lines into circles, first together then apart, first closed then open, and we waltzed and glided and laughed, holding tight to the night's crisp shine. We stopped for a while, rested on the bank, not even feeling the cold, just feeling alive to the life that was without us and within us, brilliantly, sharply, and brightly alive to it all. We rose, we started again and swirled gently outward this time, slowing ourselves to music hummed from our lips, pacing ourselves to the deepening night, catching glimpses reflected from the river's glazed surface, from whose silvery surface came glimpses of unmarked depth. We whirled slowly, twirled and bent our bodies to one another, swirled our faces back and forth each before the other. The ice beneath us hummed back with each gentle cut; we swayed and swirled and hummed, keeping perfect rhythm with ourselves. And then I felt the warmth without me, a warm wet that came from deep within, liquid and soft, humming its way toward my thighs. It was warm, so warm and so soft. And then there were warm lumps, wet lumps, several wet lumps that came out of my thighs, coursed into my knees and took us down onto the ice. A yawning gulf opened out of which flew shapes I could not name. He kept saying my name but it had no relation to me. My outer thighs, my buttocks now numb with cold; the middle of my legs, my female center still warm with blood.

We were together last night for the first time since I lost the baby. But, oh God, I swear that he shivered.

Hawthorne: a shrub with stiletto thorns.
Peabody: a body, bloated, with pea head.

What terribly sharp, deformed thing have we birthed?

I have discovered that the journal we were keeping together has disappeared. I do not ask about it. It is burned, I know. He has fired many pages other than these.

Lizzie

Herman shivers so with the cold. His soul must be bruised, he shakes so. It is almost contagious, this cold violence of his. He did not used to be always like this but is becoming increasingly so. I feel it most after he has returned from being abroad with Hawthorne. I am sure he has told no one about us but I do not know then why my husband returns so.

Sophia

The garden is so wonderfully prolific that we eat like kings no matter that we have so very little money. The soil here is richer than any we had ever seen; it teems so with energy and fertile life that it is deepened into a brown that is black. I do take delight in looking out and seeing the pots filled with my Cuban flowers; just before our marriage I took seeds and carried them with me here. On West Street they filled me with delight and fond remembrance; here, now, they still fill me with those but they fill me with something else too, making me feel so full that I want to open my mouth to let it out and cannot. Fill me so full that I begin to bloat and float and get unanchored from the earth and feel as if I am about to float out of and beyond my self in this world. If I were to paint what it is that now fills me I would stretch my canvas taut, figure a knife handle in the center of the canvas, the joint of the blade and handle smooth with the canvas. The blade would not be visible. Yet again I might take a canvas and not stretch it smooth at all. Leave folds—folded ripples—across the surface instead. And then I would take my brush and I would mix together orange and blue and emerald and I would paint flames across its breadth. And then I would hold the canvas in my hands, hold it taut and then relax; hold it taut and then relax, with such speed that the colors would dance right out of the room.

My language worries me.

I have discovered some terrible words that I cannot undiscover, though I have certainly tried. I came across a letter that he had written to his sister Louisa in which he describes our marriage. I was cleaning out the cupboard in the parlor and found it, opened, lying atop a stack of papers. The ink cuts into my flesh even as I read the words, even now as I recall them. He wrote—and I quote precisely, verbatim— "The execution is complete." There is more that follows of an admittedly different tone, but it does not take away the awfulness of those words. Not even when he says that then we traveled to the Manse and found Paradise there. I cannot see how an execution can pave the way to Paradise. These words have guillotined me.

Lizzie

He rages, at night. Bellow upon bellow from downstairs. His words find me, no matter how far I go. When they reach me they are but echoes, hollow, empty yet full of rage still. And bitter. More bitter than hemlock every dared to be. He finds me dull. I do not excite him. No wonder he joined a penis with a cassock. That was his revelation, what he had when his god left him. A holy fright, I call it. He terrifies me. To be wed to that all these years—well, now I share his morbid excitement.

Sophia

I have managed to find time to create a little still life out of shells. It is quite the thing these days. The last issue of Godey's had complete instructions; Mallard's in town had the shells, the glass globe under which they will be preserved, and all the other necessary items. I pretended that I would sell it and so justified spending so much money for the materials. It is a fancy thing—fancy in the extreme. It is nearly eight inches high and almost as wide; it is an exotic landscape all contained on one branch. And it is well preserved under sealed glass. It literally teems with blossoms and buds and thorns and vines—the kind that surely can live only in the imagination. Not even in Cuba did I see such things. And they are so knotted together that not even I can tell where one starts and another begins. No one else even has the faintest idea what it is. But that is no matter.

Lizzie

Sophia talked yesterday at length about Jane Eyre. I like Jane but it's Grace Poole that intrigues me. There is no grace in her—she's a woman. But Poole is right—she will drown in her own likeness. Worse yet, she'll be like Pip, trapped in his blasted black body without his forty dollar soul, slave to a crazy master.

Sophia

I have spent the last week stealing as much time as I can from the household and the children and my husband. Connie brought back from her latest travels a book by Emily Bronte. It is called *Wuthering Heights*. Connie said that it was not very popular and she herself had not had time to read it but thought I might find time. I must admit that I was skeptical. I don't have time to read and if I did I would want to read a book that had some reputation. But open the cover I did. And, alas, it has been, I guess, what I could call my undoing. I swear that I understand the very soul of Heathcliff. Oh, to be buried together but with the covers of the coffins removed so that their flesh could rot and flow into one entity apart from all humanity. With covers off, they would become one thing, created out of two separate roots.

Lizzie

If I were Lulu Elizabeth Yellowbird Many Stars Hawkridge Hitch-cock I too would become Lizzie Cock and find many stars at my feet. And then I would climb to the highest mountain on the earth, slip off my moccasins and squish my toes into the ground and reach so high that I could pull the stars down and place them in a bag at my waist. Never again would I feel dwarfed.

Sophia

We have been to hear Thoreau speak on life in New England. It has been a cold, drear November day and the evening has deepened into a sharp, brittle cold that promises deep snow. I fear that I have been most unkind and ungenerous to him; I honestly confess that I do not think I could see past his terribly uncomely nose, not even when he had so generously prepared the garden for us at the Manse. But his voice changed his face for me forever. To hear him speak this evening gave me faith that he was not arrogant after all. His great, large blue eyes voiced the depth of heart he brought to his philosophy. The lecture was so enchanting, such a revelation of nature in all its exquisite details of wood-thrushes, squirrels, sunshine, mists and shadows, fresh, vernal odors, and pine-tree ocean melodies that my ears sang with the ring of music. It seemed as if it was a May afternoon and I had been wandering through copse and dingle. I have also written this description—or something very like it—in a letter. I use there, I believe, some of the very same figures of speech and maybe even some of the same sentences. But there I did not add this. I shall look forward to his next visit and not pretend to be absorbed in the laundry as I used to do.

Yellowbird

presses

her

feet

Into the earth.

With her toes,

Yellowbird

Traces

The ridged outlines of her scarred face.

Yellowbird turns her toes inward

Yellowbird turns her toes outward

Shaping her world

herself.

Lizzie

The old-timers believed that John Hawkridge Hitchcock came very close to Yellowbird. He was in a grove so deep and tangled that he couldn't get out. He couldn't get to its center but instead got trapped in its perimeter, endlessly tracing and retracing the same steps for years on end. For six months of every year he moaned and for six months of every year he laughed, holding on to Lulu's bag all the while.

Sophia

My husband's mother died yesterday after a terrible siege. Pains so extreme they heaved her from the bed. So extreme they emptied her. She would open her mouth and nothing would come. She would be an open, gaping hole from which came no sound to give shape to her terrible pain. I would hold her; the force of that pain would lift both of us from the bed. She died in my arms. He was not there.

The doctor says that he has brain fever. He does not get out of his bed. He has the shape of an invalid, I fear. He has the look of death upon him. His skin is ashen; his eyes have sunk nearly into his cheekbones. They have a look to them that I can neither describe nor imagine how to paint. It is as if they have not just seen hell; it is, I swear, as if they are hell.

He is finally much improved though he still looks into a haunted depth. I can tell. When he got out of bed this morning, he hunched over, holding his stomach so tightly that his knuckles became white. When he finally straightened up and looked toward me, I saw a blank where his face used to be.

I have spent so much time gazing at the spider's web outside my window that I have not been able to get a line from Marvell out of my mind. "Insnared with flowers, I fall on grass." I keep imaging this very disturbing picture of vines that have become hairy threads that have wound themselves around my ankles and then back and forth between and around my legs until they have sewn me shut.

Lizzie

"You're the reason, goddamned you. Goddamned you to hell. It wasn't me. It was you—you, all along. You. Malcolm. My son. He killed himself to get away from you. You and your constant sniveling and complaining and sickness. Sick. Sick. All the time, you're sick. Stuffed up like a goddamned dead bird. I should roast you. Do you hear me? I should R-O-A-S-T you. Tough, stringy, rotten, sick—not even worth bothering with roasted and dead. You worthless squaw. He couldn't stand the no-good Indian in him. You just live with that, you damned rotten bird beak of a black squaw. My son's dead because of you—you and your goddamned black Indian heart. Goddamned you to hell, he's dead."

They said it was because of his grief that he spoke so. Hah! Pretty to think so. I will call his book an incubus, you'll see. But his tongue—oh that is a dreadful incubus indeed. I wish I could tell Sophia—she must know what it is like for she lives with one too. I am sure she does.

Sophia

I went to his study. I knocked. He did not answer. I knocked again. I opened the door, despite the silence. I imagined myself at the Manse, and began to dance, just as if I was Salome all over again, leading him into the medallioned carpet, the one that whirlwinded you right off the ground. I touched the feathers of my hat and dipped low in front of him so that he could see his image caressed by the soft fingers of the plumes. He took my shoulders. Raised me to him. Set his eyes dead center, meeting mine. He began to walk me but not towards him, not walking that would soon become a sweep off the floor. He walked me backwards, endlessly it seemed, toward the door. And then I was placed through the door, over its threshold. When it closed in my face there was no garland of acanthus. I faced a blank, dark, panel of wood, reflecting nothing in its simply beaded frame.

Lizzie

I stand in front of the looking glass trying to recover myself. I have aged; I have become frail. But I can still see in my eyes the life I should have had. My hair has thinned; my teeth have yellowed. But my eyes are still brilliantly hazel, the color of walnuts and moss combined. They even have, I believe, hints of blue and red and black. Speckled eyes. Intricate eyes, I say.

The door latch lifts. I smell him before I see him. He has been abroad again, at the Inns, with the men.

"What the hell you just standing there for, like some idiot?" he growls.

"I was just thinking," I say, raising my arms, just in case.

"Thinking? You thinking? What the hell do you have to think about?" As he lurched forward he burped "excuse me."

Before I could move out of the way, he bolted in front of me, with his back to me. He filled the glass; his face replaced mine. His eyes, angry, sullen, frightful, reflected back. He moved to within an inch of the glass. I kept looking straight ahead. All I could see now was the back of his head, his hair matted and soiled.

"Now there's thinking that's worth something," he yelled as he drew his hands through the top and sides of his hair, holding it straight out, creating a strange and hairy halo effect. "There," he bellowed as he began to pull and tug at his hair. I began to back out, as noiselessly as possible, grateful that I had begun always to carry keys in my pocket. I locked the door behind me.

Bellow after bellow, he raged for six hours. The glass shattered; objects were flung. When all sound stopped, I unlocked the door. He was asleep, on the floor, with his knees curled up to his nose.

"The bastard has pissed his pants again," I hiss.

I want to stab him. But I rouse him, help undress him, and put him to bed. But I'll be damned if I clean him up this time, I vow.

Sophia

Melville comes to visit often and they go for long walks together. I am very glad for my husband that he has this friendship and these walks. But what walking I do is with the children. Almost never do I go abroad. And my husband and I have not gone together in years. And yet he is writing very well.

I do, however, often go into the yard from which rise the Berkshire mountains and I imagine myself making their ascent. I imagine myself lost in the mazes of their slopes, threading my way through the barriers of the underbrush, arriving at meadows whereupon I stretch wide and long and then lay open to the wind, parting my legs into a wide inverted V and then rising and jumping over the streams that are like openwork through the treed fabric of the land. And I imagine my hands upon the rocky slopes, shiny with mica and dark with traces of shale. I feel the hard edges jut into my palms and I am aware of a softness that sighs.

Elizabeth sent up a few new pamphlets that have been circulating about Boston. It is amazing to me what some people are willing to believe. One says that if we are to have pure souls then we must dress ourselves in white and eat only foods that are white—or, they do allow, those that are tinged with a bit of yellow or pink. All I could see as I read this is a plate filled with potatoes and turnip and rutabaga swimming in milk gravy and then so mixed up together that there was nothing left but a mashed-up lump.

Melville called earlier; he did not know that my husband had gone into Boston to call upon his publishers since they have answered no letters inquiring about the money owed. I invited him in, but, as it so chanced, he invited me out since Mrs. Hotchkiss had happened by and said that it would do me good to go out and get some fresh air and she would enjoy staying with the children. Without even realizing it, we walked the entire afternoon. It was not until we felt the light of day begin to give way that we headed home.

This man has a power that I cannot account for. We talked of many things this day, some of which I have already forgotten and some of

111

which I shall never be able to forget. He has been at furious work upon his book, some of which I have heard about third-hand. He seemed, at first, shy and embarrassed and apologized more than once if he was boring me with this tale about a mammoth white whale. I admit that when it became clear to me that the conversation had indeed taken an irrevocable turn to the whale I was not overcome with enthusiasm. But soon that changed—rapidly and irrevocably, I'm afraid.

I cannot find words adequate to my feeling. It was as if his voice gave shape to words that were in me rather than coming from him. It was as if he formed the very thoughts that had been trying to form in my brain but that my hands couldn't fashion. It was as if the tale he began to spin was --well, not the thread that I had been trying to grasp but proof that that thread existed. We walked and he talked, sketching out fragments of pictures of this creature, fragments that have been reshaping themselves in me ever since. He would say a word and then I would begin to create pictures until I wasn't even hearing his words anymore and then I would hear his words and revise the very picture I had just spun into view and then I would see his lips moving but not hear a sound and yet spin more pictures anyway. I have never heard a human voice give such power to a word that hasn't even a shape upon a page.

Much later I realized that not once had I even thought of the children.

Later yet I knew that his voice is a grand hooded phantom that licks the mountains in my eye.

Lizzie

Hawthorne has come yet again. I know this should stop and yet I can't convince myself that it really should. I can't say that I really like being with him but I can't say that I really don't either. It isn't frightful as it is with Herman but there is something vacant about him during it that makes me shiver.

I keep thinking about what he wrote in one of his stories. That all simple emotions are blessed. And that it's the lurid intermixture of things that's so awful. Hah—he has no idea, I am sure, of what a real lurid intermixture is. He has bedded down with one and doesn't even know it.

And just like that it all comes to me in a horror. It's not me he wants after all. I'm just the closest he thinks he can get. It's not me—it's him. And oh god, all of a sudden, I understood what had really gone on in those hills. He was no longer a white, blank, featureless thing. I know the tattoo he should have. A large mouth, colored red and black, that screams open and shuts as tight as a vise every time he moves.

I say that to my self, letting my mouth open wide and clamp down, loving how it all feels on my tongue, my lips.

Goddamned, Lizzie old girl, I tell myself, this is better than buried hair.

-Yellowbird-

Yellowbird has many visions. And she hears drums, many drums. Drums of change. Drums of death. Drums of life lived, life relived, life yet to be lived. She watches Sophia wince at the sight of her nephew enroll in the army. He is in the fife and drum corps. He wears tattered pants with rolled cuffs. He wears a dress hat many sizes too big for his small head. He tilts his head back to see; he hunches his shoulders forward to try to keep the hat from falling off backwards. The weight of the drum pushes his chest forward. He has all he can do to keep his balance.

Yellowbird watches him march forward, trying his best to keep time, trying his hardest to stay in tune with his fellow soldiers. He is proud of the drum he carries; he imagines it the best drum in the world. The top and bottom are fine-grade calfskin, stretched taut over the wooden body. Across the bottom are strung bands of cattle gut; he can loosen or tighten these to control the sound.

He imagines himself a wild warrior fighting for his freedom, for his people. This boy/man is set for sacrifice; his eyes speak nothing as he looks straight ahead, marching away from his former life. He dares not look back; he holds his body as straight as he can, already cursing the weight of the rifle at his side. He misses a beat; he knows that he will not return. He is set for sacrifice.

Sophia watches him recede against the horizon, become but a moving speck, ever smaller, ever more far away. When she turns to begin her walk home she is reminded of ants and spiders and things. She laughs uneasily as she remembers how easily they fall beneath her feet.

Yellowbird hears the boy/man drumming. His beat is not deep; it does not shake the earth. His is, alas, but a domestic sound, destined to

114

die out silently in the rush of life.

Yellowbird hears, too, the drums of condemnation. She remembers when Pond Lily commits incest; she feels again the horror, the pain of the extermination that follows. She can feel Pond Lily bite the pattern into the bark chain her husband is condemned to wear around his neck; she can feel the weight of it as Dark Raven places it around his neck, aware that it condemns him to life. Yellowbird must relive this from beginning to end.

The tribal elders meet and decide that Dark Raven must walk the earth alone, must live by himself, ever bearing his wife's bitten patterns. The rest of her tribe must extinguish themselves; Pond Lily has made it impossible for them to survive, lest they breed another like her. They will all go separate ways, and be absorbed into other tribes. After much deliberation, the tribal council decides to combine all known tribal rituals into one sufficiently strange and complex to carry the weight of her deed.

Pond Lily and Dark Raven are made to join hands and dance in a circle, singing songs of death and desire. They each have been given a mask made of bark; each mask has been painted with the face of a beast so strange it resembles no known creature on earth. With each pass around the circle Yellowbird swears she can see the beast-face change. Sometimes she sees only a huge mouth; then again only huge eyes; and then again nothing but a wild mane. They are made to dance faster and faster until both appear mesmerized, in a trance, galloping around and around, feet barely touching the ground, heads thrown back and forth, flinging off ropes of saliva that spill forth from their mouths as they yell the songs of death and desire.

They fall to the ground. Pond Lily's mother is the one who must first take off their beast-masks and replace them with the tassel mask, painted boldly with ripe kernels. It is the way it should be; the corn has germinated, grown big, and now the husk must die. The pair must repeat the dancing and the singing until once again, mesmerized, exhausted, they fall to the ground. Pond Lily's father must take off their tassel masks and replace them with the mask with no face. It is blank. Simply and terribly blank. Even the natural grain of the bark has been stripped clean;

115

it has been pounded smooth. Eyes searching it find nothing. Fingers running over it find nothing.

Pond Lily and Dark Raven complete this third dance and song, falling once again. This time no one changes the mask. Pond Lily is brought a very large, strong piece of bark. She takes it, folds it in many layers, then brings it to her mouth under the mask, and bites the entire surface. She removes it, mask still intact, unfolds the bark, feeling the pattern she has inscribed with her teeth. She is confident that it is the sky with all the stars in the wrong places.

Pond Lily's mother and father bring their daughter's hand to Dark Raven; his hand is placed over hers and the transfer of the chain is complete. Dark Raven knows he must stand, mask in place and chain on neck, for two days while Pond Lily and her tribe disappear. He is then free to live, alone, ever wearing her bite at his throat.

Pond Lily's brother, Sharp Claw, has been erased from the earth.

Yellowbird hears the drum of memory beating loudly and wildly in her breast. It is stretched taut, top and bottom, with the finest elk hide her grandfather could find. Its circular sides are of the strongest oak, carved with the beak of the eagle and the wing of the hawk. The whole is laced together with the guts of a cougar; as grandfather loosens or tightens the catgut, he changes the sound he makes. Yellowbird can still feel the vibrations; when he played that drum, the earth shook a deep, reverberating song.

Sophia

We will never, I am afraid, be able to reassemble our original group for conversations. News arrived, terrible in its tragedy and in its irony. Margaret and her family were forced to leave Italy because of the revolution. She was in the midst of gathering material but did not have enough money to stay abroad. The work will never be finished. She and her husband and son were almost home. But their ship sank just off the coast of Long Island at Fire Island. How bitter the ironies. She relished the very idea of revolt and here it helped her to her death. And to drown off of fire island—oh, the very sound of it makes me feel the terrible force of the waves lapping at her throat. And in sight of land, no less. How much more bitter the irony. I am only glad that she had found some happiness near the end. It is a measure of her power, I think, that so many have derided her marriage, her work, her life. But we have known her power, felt the mystical pulse of her words. So often our conversations would end when she, exhausted and exhilarated by the talk of the evening, would begin to slip from our parlor world into a room in a house that we could not see but in which we could feel her presence reside. She was, in effect, in a trance. Her eyes were distant but vividly alive; the words she would occasionally utter we could not decipher the literal meaning of. But there was no mistake that the sound that came from her throat had its genesis in something invisible to us. I admit she was brash and, like Elizabeth, too adamant in her opinions. But she contained a mountain inside her. There is no one I know that had more depths and peaks than she did. When she spoke you knew that even her whisper could deepen the meaning of any word that passed through her lips.

Lizzie

"The fact is, that Herman, poor fellow, is in such a frightfully nervous state, & particularly now with such an added strain on his mind. That I am actually *afraid* to have any one here for fear he will be upset entirely, & not be able to go on with the printing—He was not willing to have even his own sisters here. . . . If ever this dreadful *incubus* of a book . . . gets off Herman's shoulders I do hope he may be in better mental health--but at present I have reason to feel the gravest concern & anxiety about it--to put it in mild phrase. . . ." —Lizzie Shaw Melville, letter to her mother

Sophia

Elizabeth told me something about Margaret that disturbed me deeply. She had written from Italy that "It is very sad that we have no money, we could be so quietly happy a while." I am so bothered by a number of things. Quietly happy—somehow I cannot reconcile my vision of her with this. It could be the image of domestic contentment, I am sure. But coming from those lips, from the depths of that throat, it seems to me that this human mountain knew that there was no earthly space large enough to contain her loud happiness. And even then, when she was married and had had a child, even then the poisoned milk and wine were never out of her taste's reach. So quietly happy a while— even this diminished happiness would be hers but a while. That diligent heart that wrote itself across pages to the very end. And only to have her last manuscript lost at sea, torn leaf by leaf into the waves, erased line by line by the water that sucked from her her very breath.

Alas, the black haircloth rocker she gave us is broken. One of its rockers is broken in three places, I am afraid. It sits in the shed at the back of the house, awaiting resurrection.

Lizzie

My fingertips bleed so. I am not very adept at managing these quills. The barbs stab me, no matter how quickly I try to get my flesh out of the way. I have to knot my fingers better; I have to wet the barbs more. But I will learn. I'll use my teeth, I vow.

I say to myself I am no harpooned whale, waiting for slaughter. I laugh. And even if I am, I assure myself, I'll bring down the damned ship with me.

Just then I had a vision of Lizzie Cock and Lulu Hawkridge Hitchcock on top of a mountain capturing the eagle that had made off with Lulu's bag.

Sophia

I was so certain that it was but a noisome fly and I was thoroughly annoyed that it landed on my arm where I could feel its mossy-haired legs needle into my skin. Without thought, I squashed it, violently, with my hand, not caring that I would dirty my entire palm with its carcass. But an instant afterward it came to me in a flash. It was not a fly. It was a tiny winged creature, an exquisite miniature of a little winged world. In a flash, I saw the world reflected through the translucent pattern of its wings. But my hand was so much more quick than my eye. In a flash, I destroyed that translucent gate through which I might have passed into another room of the world.

There has been so much in the paper of late about the enlarged Capitol and the grand ceremonies held there over Independence Day. President Fillmore has laid yet another cornerstone. There was, of course, the original one, and then the one that was laid years later after it was rebuilt having been burned by the British during the War of 1812. And now it has been enlarged, so yet a third cornerstone is now placed. Daniel Webster made a dedication speech for the occasion. I usually take little note of such political ceremony but I have remarked this one. If the Capitol is burned again, how many cornerstones would be placed? And if there are more additions, will more cornerstones be placed? And if there were many many cornerstones, so that the building becomes an endless series of added-on wings, what will it be like to thread one's way through these angular passages? When President Washington, who acted as both President and a Mason for the event, laid the first one it was inscribed with dates. I think it was something like 4, for it being the fourth year of his presidency; 13, since it was the thirteenth year of the United States, and 5917, it being the Masonic year. I wonder if this is prophetic and the wings of the capitol shall grow so large that it will become a beast whose visage and girth not even a Daniel Webster could name.

Lizzie

No one knew for sure when Lizzie Cock Too Melville first arrived but there she was in Boston, the new bride of my son Malcolm. He loved her, that much is clear. He wrote:

"My dearest Lizzie:

My own Lizzie. I can hardly believe that I can say that. It was paradise indeed when you said yes, that you would be my wife. I pledge that I will always cherish you and keep you first in all things.

My own wife: What a thrilling sound that is! I love to say that and can hardly wait until I return this evening. In Paradise's very bower is where we will be. I blush to think how happy we are there.

You dearest, ownest husband, Malcolm."

How did it ever come to pass that he put a bullet through his head on their third anniversary? She was downstairs, ready to ascend; he had gone upstairs, he said, to wait for her. She heard the shot; it shook the house; it pierced her ears and heart.

When she reached the top of the stairs she saw him, lying on the floor at the foot of the bed. His brains had splattered on the wall. The bed was clean.

Sophia

I have been reading Melville's book and it is very, very powerful. But the words on the page do not capture, I think, the full power that is behind them. But there are phrases and places that do come so close. To recollect the glimpse of it that I felt that afternoon is both thrilling and frightening. I do not think my husband could write such a book.

Perhaps I should not have written that. But I do not think that it is a mistake. I do not think that I will correct it.

Lizzie

Pecker's best story is about her father during the war. He didn't fight; he was too old and scared. All Hiram could do about it was sit in his room, cross-legged, and think. He looked at his woolen, hounds-tooth-checked robe, emptied and formless, hanging over the chair. He got up, took the robe, went to the kitchen. He got the bottle and the shears, drank from the bottle and lay the robe across his knees. He drank again, raised the robe to the table and spread it out in front of him. He drank again, took the shears, and cut the expanse before him into strips, not even, regular strips but strips of all various sizes, all sorts of widths and lengths. When he finished cutting, he gathered all the strips into a pile before him. And then, with slow deliberation and serious intent, he arranged and rearranged his strip troops, planning every battle of the war, making strip troops and strip people, according to his plan.

Buster had lain awake too—he too was old and scared. He heard Hiram in the kitchen; he got up after a bit to see what Hiram was doing. He saw Hiram at the table, with strips of hounds-tooth all around, and asked "what the hell are you doing?"

"I'm planning," Hiram answered, exasperated. "Can't you see that?"

Buster couldn't. "Plannin' what?"

"How loyalty wins the war," Hiram countered.

"By cuttin' up a robe and puttin' it on a table?" Buster asked, incredulously.

"Nope, you damned fool. By making pieces out of a whole."

Buster thought a moment, wondering whether this was as good a time as any for telling the truth.

"Sorry, Hiram, but I don't reckon you know nothing about any of these things."

"And you do, I suppose?"

"I know lots. Lots more than you might think."

"So what? That make you Jesus or something?" spat Hiram.

"Hiram, do you remember those horses and that wagon I come down to your place with a few years ago, when you let me stay on after Ruth died? The ones I said weren't mine?"

"Course I do."

"Well, they weren't what I said."

"Weren't they?"

"Nope, they was mine alright," Buster admitted, sitting down at the table.

Hiram didn't answer. He shifted troops.

"They was," continued Buster. "And that's why I couldn't keep them."

"Now what the hell kind of craziness is that? And you said you were looking at a crazy man," Hiram admonished.

"Cause if I'd a kept them, it would have been just like giving them to you. You know, like payment or something," Buster admitted.

"I guess I can see how it would have been like that, maybe." Hiram shifted more troops.

"I guess you probably think that I owed 'em to you, don't you?"

"Don't owe me nothin', I reckon."

Buster stood up. "You're wrong, Hiram. Real wrong."

Hiram took up a whole line of pieces that he had set apart, scooped them into one loose bundle, and let them filter through his fingers.

Buster continued, pacing as he spoke. "I owed you enough not to give you those horses or that wagon neither."

Hiram took up another, smaller handful and let them fall too.

"Hiram, I just couldn't do it. Couldn't give them to you. It might have made us think we was even."

Buster came to the table, picked up a piece and placed it by Hiram's hand.

After Buster left, Hiram picked up the piece, placed it away from him, picked it up again, and held it. "Damned fool. World's full of them," he said, shaking his head. He picked up the piece again, placed it back in line, defending the right rear from attack.

Hiram saw himself in uniform, cutting across enemy lines. He knew he should clean his tracks but he didn't give a damn about being followed. When he was sure that he had won enough and saw a clear way to win the rest, he left the field.

Sophia

As you know, I have ever been pondering the scene between Ophelia and Hamlet that is at the very center of the drama. I read the scene aloud three times. Perhaps it is because the words come from the mouth of a woman who has given birth. I do not know for certain, but the words assumed a shape, a meaning that they had never had before. "Get thee to a nunnery. Why wouldst thou be a breeder of sinners? I am myself indiffferent honest, but yet I could accuse me of such things that it were better my mother had not borne me: I am very proud, revengeful, ambitious, with more offenses at my beck than I have thoughts to put them in, imagination to give them shape, or time to act them in. What should fellows such as I do crawling between earth and heaven? We are errant knaves, all; believe none of us. Go thy ways to a nunnery." It is not until now that I have begun to see the shape that is these words. His words of supposed love—that Ophelia believed to be true and which he now admonishes her are not to be believed—are the very knave that would make her the breeder of sinners. It is the words that are but an analogy for the organ of love that would generate such offspring and it is because of the analogy that the offspring must be tainted with sin. So, poor Hamlet, realizing that he must practice deceit with his language—making it ambiguous when he intended none—sees himself as the taker of her virtue and in desperation sends her from him to the only place where she will be safe from his mouth. His words, then, can impregnate her with tragedy. Oh, how I could have never felt any of this before, I do not know. Only now do I begin to see what it is that he has seen, is seeing. He sees himself—his words, his body—contaminated; he cannot imagine that he will not spread it to she that he does truly love.

But I still do not see—cannot envision—what it is that she has seen, is seeing.

Lizzie

Hawthorne did it to Hester. He gave her some real life but then he tames her—no, worse than that. He suffocates her, damned it, drowns her, not with water but with a letter. She doesn't speak; he has taken her voice. Buster maybe had something after all. The ghosts that come, with their hatchets and tomahawks, are not very different from the ones who write women into submission, who exterminate their real nature.

Sophia

Christmas is fast approaching and I know that the children will be getting so many, many toys. And I doubt that Una will ever care whether the lion is saved or not. Elizabeth gave it to her when she was born, even though we did not know whether Una would survive. A large, stuffed, ferocious-looking lion that was almost as big as she. But oh how Una clutched tight to it, teethed it, and later walked with it throughout the house. Its head is almost threadbare and it has not been held for so very long. But I could not throw it away, even when none of the other children showed any interest in it. But I am going to recover it and I am going to begin it tomorrow.

I have plenty of fabrics already cut at hand. But when I looked at them, none seemed to fit the lion, at least not in the way I imagined him stuffed. So I went to the shed, despite the bitter cold wind that passes through its northeasterly face. The fabric on the bottom of the rocker would fit. It was just worn enough, with still enough serviceable life left in it but without such disquieting newness that it would never fit the old stuffed frame as it should. This fabric had the contours of life upon it; I was sure that I could recover a lion's face lined with the crevices of living. I lifted easily the welting cord around the perimeter of the seat. I carefully began to pry out each tack, careful not to the tear the fabric even though it bore no resemblance to the fabric I wanted. Having been hidden under the cord, it did not show the wear that the rest of the seat did. I thought that when I had pried loose just enough of the tacks I would begin to see the horsehair padding release from its confining frame, bounce outward and reassume its shape, becoming full enough to fill the empty spaces inside the lion. But it does not move. It is matted down. The entire seat is off, but it remains flat. Completely flat. I place the fabric back over the seat. I do not tack it down. There is no need.

He has been prolific of late, with the third novel in as many years. But I sense that there is something different about this one and not just because he has set it at Brook Farm. He has read to me sections of his draft, as he usually does, but he has not, oddly, included the parts I find most interesting. I have read more than he realizes, and find that something puzzles and troubles me. I would say nothing, of course—and he certainly did not ask, anyway—of his characterization of Zenobia. I am troubled. Her fleshy flower is turned into a cold and hard jewel that reflects too harshly. I know that she resembles Margaret and I suspect that most readers will see the likeness. But I think she resembles far more poor Elizabeth and I suspect that few readers will see that likeness. Even fewer that her cold spark could only come from Lizzie. I am sure of it. He did not ask so I did not tell him that my favorite section has been when Zenobia shuts the curtain on her cold observer. I know my husband would not be pleased. It does not matter as I do not think he will ask for my opinion. If I were to paint her life, she would become the spirit of the water and not its victim.

At least I like to think that I would.

Lizzie

Sometimes I do not think he is human, he talks so. Hell is not a place, I am sure. It's a sound. It's your name come straight from the howling mouth of a beast. "Lizzzzzzzeeeeeee," he snorts. He paws me. "Lizzzzzzzzzzzzzzzzzzzzeeeeeeeeeeeeeee deeaarrr," he snorts again, expecting to mount me, ram me once more. I dart from the bed, run to the study and lock the door. He wails and pounds but the door is strong. I have no fear.

-Yellowbird-

Yellowbird often tells of the giant who reached up, took the sun, and buried it. The world shivered in the darkness, wrapped in a cold shroud, waiting and praying for death. But Grandfather and Grandmother fought back.

They picked their three strongest, bravest men and sent them to dig a hole deep enough so they could recover the sun. They dug for many days and nights, carving out a hole so deep that even an echo could not reach its bottom. They dug so deep they fell into another world, just disappearing from this one. No one has ever heard or seen them since.

They then sent their three strongest, bravest women who dug even deeper. Not only did they break through into the next world but they also broke through into yet another. People swear that you can hear an echo from that world into this one. Some swear that it sounds like an open-mouthed Aaaaahhhhhhh.

Then they sent their strangest child, a hermaphrodite that lives by itself. The minute it was weaned, it was made to live in a teepee on the margins of the tribal ring, fed in turns by each member of the tribe. It was forbidden to speak to the child or to hold it. It was forbidden to say its name. But it was demanded that everyone feed it.

The child set out not to dig a hole but to find the sun-burying giant. Just as the child set out, a yellow and white cat appeared. Yellow like corn. White like clouds. The cat reminded the child of the taste of honey. So he/she calls it Corn Clouds, Sweet Stuff.

Corn Clouds, Sweet Stuff and Too Many Parts travel for many days before they find the giant. When they do, they bite into his ankles and hold tight. They will not let the giant shake them, even though the whole earth shudders with his kicking. The Sun-buryer kicks so hard and so long into the earth trying to dislodge them that he opens up a hole deep and wide enough to hold the sun. With a last kick, the world hears a huge rush of wind as the sun shoots from the earth and recovers its place in the sky.

They found the child and the cat curled together, limp and heavy with what seemed life. They stayed that way for days. When they were finally stiff and rigid, a platform was tied between two trees, and the tribes of the world gathered. Grandmother and Grandfather gathered the-now-stiff-but-still-curled-together child and cat and placed them on the platform. After they were burned, Grandmother and Grandfather gathered their ashes and mixed them together.

Grandmother and Grandfather carry the ashes in a rawhide pouch around their ankles, tied in such a way that they touch the tops of their moccasined feet. Each pouch is inscribed with an eagle so that when they walk the eagles fly.

Sophia

I must write this down. A few nights ago I had a wonderful dream. I dreamed of the mourning picture that hung in mother's parlor. But it was I who was the black-and-white clothed figure and I could feel the cold, sharp edge of the granite ledge upon which I rested my wearied shoulder. I felt chilled, and alone, and desolate, as if something had been wrenched from the inside of me, leaving a space emptied of even the possibility of it ever being filled again. Just as I felt my mouth begin to open and a howlish sound begin to fly out, I felt a soft hand at my back, resting on my shoulder, turning the granite ledge into a softly flamed lap into which I let myself down. The canopied willow tree in the background had stepped forth into the foreground, surrounded and enveloped me in its leafy, tendrilled arms, embracing me with the mossy warmth that hung from its limbs.

This morning, as I was trying to imagine how I would paint this scene, how I would move the willow's drooping branches to the foreground, the chasm that is in that other picture began to open and began to swallow all of the foreground of that picture and now the one that I thought was mine and I felt the lapping lips of the crevice close round me. I reached for the willow, to grab one of its branches, to gain a hold against the widening space. But I could not reach any of the branches. They moved further away, until the willow was no longer even in the background. It had disappeared outside the frame of the scene.

But it is this evening that I am afraid of. As I tried to remember the warmth of my recreated picture, of the soft embrace of the mossy tips of the leaves, it came to me in a flash that the soft touch of the willow leaves against my neck were the soft sighs of the incubi who so long ago began to try to suck the life out of me. And, my God, I realize that I am being nailed down into such a narrow space that there is not even room enough to fit a dead, drained, matted-down me.

Lizzie

I can't get Beatrice Cenci out of my mind. She is innocent—I am sure of it. I just wonder she didn't kill him sooner. But she has grounds—he is her father. I have no grounds—he is my husband. I remember, though, that her grounds didn't save her. So what is the use?

Someday I will have a knife handy. But before I do, I must quill a case for it. The case must be intricate, gorgeous, meticulous, with zigzag-stitched diamonds lined with red dots. I will hang it on my belt and wait.

Sophia

I wonder whether there could be any truth to the argument that in the days of Virgil and Horace the plants in Italy were much different than they are now. Then they supposedly bore resemblance to the alpine variety of blooms but now have assumed a much more tropical character. Perhaps the seeds of these tropical imports will escape and people Salem with their fervid spice! It is a fine, delicious thought, at any rate. I know that at some point in the future I will see Italy for myself. And when I have time to revisit Virgil and Horace then perhaps I will know whether this is true. I do suspect, though, that it is not. The author of this theory advanced it as part of his argument to continue to suppress people of dark colors lest they take over our alpine culture.

Lizzie

"I am so sorry, Lizzie, damned it, can't you see that?" As he spoke, Herman hung his head and wrung his hands, as usual. He might even cry after a while. "I didn't mean to hurt you, don't you know that? I just get crazy sometimes and do some damned crazy things but you know I don't mean them."

I made no reply. There was a time when I would have cried, believed him and had faith that he would change. But that time is gone. I have a different kind of faith now.

Sophia

I have had to let out—again, I must confess—the seams of all my dresses and skirts and undergarments. I must be more careful. I have been getting my wardrobe ready for our trip, letting out and doing over some old clothes and piecing together some new outfits, especially from the many outfits Sarah passes on to me when she is through with them. We can now afford all the cloth I could ever need but I have ever enjoyed the remaking of others' clothes into my own. I love to watch and to feel the shape I imagine from all these various fragments actually take form and become whole in my hands. I have made one spectacular outfit that I will wear on the first public excursion I will undertake in Liverpool. It is a walking dress, the likes of which has never appeared before—not even in Godey's. I will start at the top. The bonnet is of embroidered velvet, a deep moss green in color, accented by a cord of pale green satin. It is going to be banded all across the top with a garland of flowers—fresh flowers if I can procure them. If not, I have packed fabric ones that will suffice. I have sewn into the sides of the bonnet two thick pieces of cloth—each about an inch long—so that they will form a cushion that will keep it a little away from my head at all times, letting some air through.

The dress itself is fashioned out of thickly quilted, deep brown satin. I understand England is usually chilly, even in the summer, so the thickness of the fabric will provide both warmth and sufficient stiffness of form. The dress is finished at the bottom, up the front and at the ends of the sleeves with even deeper rows of quilting, imparting a lustrous quality to the whole as these deep rows catch and reflect the light differently than the less deeply drawn areas. The effect will be simple and stunning, I think, especially with the geometrical banding set against the swish of the full skirt. Of course, I will carry a parasol. It will be of the deepest, shimmering emerald green.

But I do have to be more careful. When I viewed myself in the looking glass I began to see the large, awkward shape of Elizabeth.

Lizzie

No one knew how the quill bag appeared. It contained no ashes but people swore nonetheless that it was the very same bag Lulu had carried on her journey from home. One quill from the center of a diamond was missing. Lizzie Cock Too wore the bag on her waist.

On her wedding night she took off her dress and strapped the bag around her waist. "You take me the way I am," she said. Malcolm Shaw Melville begged her to leave off the bag, complaining that the quill was rough, had sharp, tiny barbs that hurt. But he took her anyway.

Sophia

I have been reading so many wonderful novels of late, though none as good, I think, as *Jane Eyre*. Jane is such a strong and spirited girl. The image of Bertha Mason recurs to me, though, as if there is something beyond the words on the page that I want to see. I was startled, to say the least, when I read that "a quantity of dark, grizzled hair, wild as a mane, hid its head and face." I once imagined myself having drawn a canvas filled with hair, though its texture was not anything like the one that presented itself to my eyes here. Certainly this is an odd coincidence.

There are two other scenes that keep presenting themselves to me. One is Jane's own description of this purple Vampyre when she notes "the fearful blackened inflation of the lineaments." And yet a few lines later Jane reveals that this bloated face carries a "gaunt head." I am fascinated by this sharp contrast of opposing features. The other is when Jane sketches Mr. Rochester's face and then is moved to lie by claiming that it is "merely a fancy head." She describes in accurate and full detail just how she created that likeness, how she saved the eyes until last and revised her first version until the eyes were blacker and their lights flashed more brilliantly. Jane then says that she had "a friend's face under my gaze" and she "smiled at the speaking likeness." I had an odd moment of feeling uncomfortable as I read this, imagining my own portrait under the gaze of its maker. And I find that I see more than one meaning to the speaking likeness here. I must wonder whether the face under her gaze is not also her own and with what tongue it narrates itself.

"You're nothing but a goddamned Indian. A black Indian, at that," he yelled.

"Was the time, you know, you could hurt me saying that. But no more," I said, moving out of his way as I did so.

I was safe—he was so drunk he could barely stand, let alone connect with me.

"You're dead, I tell you, you're dead, rotten bird meat," he sobbed.

I was safe—he was at the crying-and-falling-down stage.

"You're a pathetic joke. Telling me I'm nobody. Who the hell do you think you are? You tried to kill me off, but couldn't. Not even with a cock at your back," I stab.

He was passed out and wouldn't remember any of it. I could say anything I imagined.

I was safe, for a time.

-Yellowbird-

Grandmother Spider told Yellowbird that there would be people on the earth who are afraid of spiders, afraid of the intricate, beautiful webs they weave. All they can see is a trap of death; all they can do is swat at it, try to break it, to destroy it. They cannot see the intricate connections; they cannot see the life that emerges from death.

Hummingbird taught Yellowbird to have faith in the invisible. Hummingbird hovered near, wings flapping so quickly they disappeared from sight. Yellowbird nodded; she knew the wings kept Hummingbird in the air, whether they were visible to her eye or not.

Grandfather Deer taught Yellowbird to walk with grace but always be ready to flee. He told her to leave an impression upon the earth as she imprinted her hoof tracks upon it but to do so gently, lovingly, always aware that these impressions are indelible. It struck Yellowbird that that was the way of all things. Once created, nothing ever disappears. Hoof tracks. Howls. Words on a page.

Sophia

We have been visiting many of the formal gardens that are so often a part of the country estates here. They are truly works of art, especially those that contain topiaries, the perfectly symmetrical knot gardens, and those wonderful maze hedges in which one can be lost for hours amidst boxwood towers shaped into perfect forms. But there is no need for fear: the feeling of ever being really lost in the wilderness is arrested by the neatly ordered border before you.

I have also discovered the most ferociously exquisite figures of a lion and lioness that I am almost certain that my descriptions will be but a very poor shadow of them. They are from the Meissen factory and are about a hundred years old, though the glaze of their hard-paste porcelain bodies retains a shiny, unbroken luster that conceals its age. Each is a separate figure; each rests on its own ormolu-mounted gilt cushion. The cushion is fascinating, held up from the ground by feet that extend from each corner, flaring out into the shape of curved fans with upturned ends. A cartouche runs underneath the long side of each base and terminates, mid-center, into a circle that touches the ground. On the top of the base—on the surface upon which these figures rest— the ground is finely etched in a series of overlapping swirls. The texture created makes one sense its relationship to some sort of grass.

The figures themselves are extraordinary. They are almost without color. The largest share of their bodies are white, relieved only by points of color on the end tufts of their tails, the ends of their toes, on their muzzles and atop their heads and on the tufts of his mane. I do not think that such a colored creature ever existed in life but there is something about them which is authentic. She has recently had cubs; her teats are engorged with milk. Both have their mouths held apart, teeth bared, tongues visible. Their necks are stretched, their shoulders and hips tensed in the final seconds before lifting themselves off their grassy pillows. Indeed, they have been molded with such exquisite care that there is a pillow of air between them and the mound of grass, a space that makes you realize that you are not safe as you view them. The only point of visible connection between them and the ground is the very tips of their claws. As you look, you imagine them lifting off; you begin to hear the roar that must issue from their open throats. But you are safe, after all. They do not ascend; they do not speak.

Lions have always elicited from me such respect and awe. I have ever had in my mind the attempt by an early New England itinerant artist to catch the visage of a great maned beast as it emerges from a tropical-looking grove of trees and bends his front half around to stare you in the face. But the likeness is all wrong, I am afraid. In the background is a bunch of pale, budded narcissus which mocks the lush thick vegetation that lies in front of the grove of trees. The beast emerges, but he is stiff—I cannot imagine that he will spring forth from his frame. His mane is wild and huge; it occupies a full third of the width and breadth of the board. His ears are small and round, rather like the size and shape of a cow. The nails with which he tries to gain a tentative hold on the ground are very long and wide and very, very black. They are so opaque that I cannot imagine that there is a network of life woven at their base. The whiskers, bright white—so unlike the subtle shadings that are natural—are short and very regularly spaced and of equal length, almost as if the artist attempted to impose a civilized order upon this wild creature. The eyes stare at you, attempt to fix you, but they cannot. They are perfectly round and composed of three circles. The outermost one is a deep, opaque black. The next is a bright white. The innermost, center one is again an opaque black. These colors and shapes do not only obscure the life in them but they also make you certain that there is no significant life there. And the muzzle, the mouth, is fascinatingly odd, strange, wrong. The lower jaw is much longer than the upper; it juts outward and curls upward over the slightly bared lower teeth. That is all you see: a row of very short, equally wide and long teeth that show no signs of wear, of natural imperfection. There is a small space between these teeth and his upper lip, which has such a deeply cleft center that it nearly touches his perfectly round and evenly-spaced nostrils. You do not have to worry about the power of his roar. From the depth of that throat there would come no words that could open and wind their lips about you.

Equally odd is that this figure is painted on a fireboard, created from three panels of what were probably cheap, knotted pine boards. The top two comprise about half the length and are of roughly equal size. The final half is of one board, over twice as wide as the upper two together. The whole of the lion figure is forced to crouch into the top two panels; only its black-toed feet extend into the bottom half. The entire landscape disappears just after the thin strip of ground, illuminated in a golden glow by slanted sunlight, which extends below the lion's feet— so thin that it occupies no more than a two-inch depth. The rest of the board, from that line downward, becomes opaque black. This figure, hunched into so small a colored space, is made to spend eternity stiffly held above a black abyss, from which he can keep himself by gripping hard a two-inch cushion of earth. If we could see under that thick fur, his knuckles would most surely be knotted a bright white. Poor thing. I cannot even imagine that the roaring flames dancing at his back can end his misery. They will not consume him, I am afraid. They will leave him perched forever above the black blankness.

Lizzie

A little port here and there has made you stout, my dear, I chuckle to myself. I am sharpening my claws, Herman dear. Beware, I say to myself as I look in the mirror. You won't ever stand in the way of me again, I vow. The black and the red of my eyes shine.

Sophia

It is now November and I do not find my eye relieved. No matter where I cast my glance, I am met with what seems a wall of solid grayness. The sun has not penetrated its thick veil for weeks. I keep imagining that these are really the great folds of draperies hung across the English stage and that at any moment the drama will begin. But, alas, though the house is full and the audience waiting, no parting comes, no sound of the human voice breaks through. I have tried to wear my most colorful outfits but, alas, to no effect. Instead of relieving the gray they seem to enhance it. So I have bought a garment partially finished and have added the embellishing touches myself. The dress is composed of horizontally striped gray taffeta. I so love taffeta; it is a fabric that has a live touch and a live sound as you hear it crackle about you. The trimmings are also of gray taffeta. The sleeves are of the horn-of-plenty shape and the shoulder trim is done with great puffings of violet taffeta. To complete the outfit is a straw bonnet trimmed with white tulle and violets.

The very front of the skirt presents a not-so-subdued demeanor. I have widened the front even more fully than it was intended. I have cut out a large inverted triangle and have divided it into five separate panels. I have studded each of these with large mother-of-pearl buttons. I have attached these at the top front of the waist. In between each of these and fitted to either side I have added panels of a slightly deeper violet taffeta, gathered and folded into horizontal bands of puffings that seem to ripple and crackle even when still. The effect is extraordinary. The length of the skirt comes to within a fraction of an inch of the ground. Because the skirt is so very, very wide, you cannot see my feet underneath. It is as if I am not attached to the earth at all and am hovering above it, floating just off its surface. This great circumferous self, as it were, is propelled across the English landscape.

I shudder to think how many layers of petticoats I would have had to wear to support this width if it were not for the cages now available. I can hardly imagine that I would have been able to walk at all, given the weight and roughness of all those horsehair petticoats. I never refer to them as crinolines—and I understand that some are referring to the cages as crinolines but I can assure you that there is a world of difference between them—even though the very sound of that word does catch something of the sharp stiffness of them against your legs. But horse-hair, it seems to me, is a much more accurate description. It makes you feel as horses must feel when they are continually bothered by flies. You keep feeling those incessant pricks against your flesh, no matter how carefully and stiffly you try to hold your legs.

Lizzie

"I think the safest course is to let her real position become apparent from the first, namely that of a wife, who, being convinced that her husband is insane, acts as if she were so convinced and applies for aid and assistance to her friends and acts with them. I think she would have done this long ago were it not for imaginary and groundless apprehensions of the censures of the world upon her conduct . . . ." —Sam Shaw, to H.W. Bellows

Of course, I write to Bellows that I continue to "pray for submission and faith." Hah! I know better. Faith can't cure it. Silly Sophia and your silly lions. Come into this parlor if you want to see a real beast.

I have seen him, eyes wild, hair standing on end, teeth bared, holding himself and rocking, rocking endlessly, violently. Crying aloud, repeatedly, "They don't like me. Goddamned it to all hell, they don't like me. They won't read a damn thing I write." Then silence, sometimes hours long. But inevitably he would rise, bash his head into the wall, over and over and over again. He keeps ramming and jamming and jamming and ramming until there is a hole and pieces of plaster fall, out of which stick barbed tufts of horsehair. And then he gallops round the perimeter of the room, endlessly, for hours on end, neighing and weeping and laughing all at once and then again in turns. Exhausted, he sinks to the floor.

In spite of myself, I almost want to comfort him.

Finally, he crawls toward his chair. He snorts, "Lizzeee, get in here. I need you. Help me, Lizzeee. Help me get up, damned it."

"Help you to hell instead," I snarl.

In spite of myself, my heart aches for him, damned it.

Sophia

Melville has spent some days here and he and my husband go walking almost every afternoon. But it is not the same as when they walked in the Berkshires and I think it more than merely being in England. When my husband returns home he is sullen, sad, discontent. I had had little chance to speak with Mr. Melville, but finally did have the opportunity I had hoped for. Ever since our talk and my subsequent reading of his novel, I have had many things I wished to ask him about. But I know my manners; I do not pry more than I think is acceptable, even though he has already confided that I have transgressed my womanhood. He put it so gently:

"My Dear Mrs Hawthorne

I have hunted up the finest Bath I could find, gilt-edged and stamped, whereon to inscribe my humble acknowledgement of your highly flattering letter of the 29th Dec: It really amazed me that you should find any satisfaction in that book. It is true that some men have said they were pleased with it, but you are the only woman for as a general thing, women have small taste for the sea . . . .
. . . Life is a long Dardenelles, My Dear Madam, the shores whereof are bright with flowers, which we want to pluck, but the bank is too high; & we float on & on, hoping to come to a landing-place at lastB-but swoop! We launch into the great sea! Yet the geographers say, even then we must not despair, because across the great sea, however desolate & vacant it may look, lie all Persia & the delicious lands roundabout Damascus.

So wishing you a pleasant voyage at last to that sweet & far coun-tree—
Believe Me Earnestly Thine—
Herman Melville"

I chose my question very carefully, having counted that this one image could provide me with clues to the answers to the rest. I asked him to go into some detail about Queequeg's tattoo—both the description of it again and the means whereby it was inscribed upon him. He gladly did so and supplied me with ample description.

"But the most important thing of it all, my dear lady, is that Queequeg wasn't your average harpooner and didn't have your average tattoos," he smiled, wickedly.

"My dear Mr. Melville, that is very clear. But what was the tattoo, exactly, and how did he come by it?" I begged.

"Well, I'll only tell you—and, of course, you will tell no one—but it was actually a foot an old Indian Squaw inscribed upon him. She put so many markings on it that nobody knew what it was."

He laughed so hard he almost choked.

Lizzie

Damn it, I know what beast rides them. Herman hates me so because I have had the man he wants. And the other one, Hawthorne, hates me because I have the man he wants. Nothing ever went on in those hills. Abandoned desire stalks them.

But this is probably just a crazy idea too. I swear that I keep hearing three male voices. They are far away, in the walls of the house, or inside the mountains, or deep within the earth. "Let us, out, please. Help, let us out," they plead.

Sometimes when I am out in the field, I swear I can feel their vibrations under my feet. Soft, insistent, far-away.

He's driving you crazy, I say to myself, and close my ears.

Sophia

I know how I would do my self-portrait. I would stretch two canvases on both sides of two separate frames, one being a fraction smaller than the other. And then I would take my knife and cut a slit down the center of one and insert the other through it so that they created a series of right angles in the round, as it were. And then I would begin to paint my figure but in order to continue it I would have to keep changing my field of vision, keep rotating myself in relation to the frame and I would follow it first across one panel and into the crevice of its angle and then outward up to and then over the edge and across yet another panel and into its crevice. I would begin to paint panels of parts, tattooed and incised with minutely detailed figures and faces and hair that flows over eight dimensions that have no beginning and no end, whose front and back bleed into one another.

Lizzie

When Sophia returns from England she will scarcely recognize me. When he is gone, I do not wear shoes. When he is gone, I put a leather belt around my waist and pull it taut. I loosen it a little; I tighten it again. I tap my sides, keeping beat with my heart. My toes grind into the carpet. I love to feel the wool fibers tickle and prick me. I squat, ready, bag at my side.

Sophia

I have had ever so much fun going abroad into the dozens of shops that line the Paris streets. I am struck by the variety of ornaments that are available. I have never before seen such variety of shawls, such exotic Indian ones, woven of rich reds and yellow and creams that they seem to flame out and warm you even before they touch you. To feel the cashmere shawls—that touch, I swear, will ever be in the tips of my fingers. There are shawls of muslin, and lace, and twilled wool and satin and silk and in every conceivable pattern and color and imaginable combination. I have never seen such variety of parasols and handbags. And not just the small ones that attach at your waist. But large, showy, ornamented ones that you carry with you and in which you carry a wealth of paraphernalia. My favorites are the long tube-shaped ones. They are of silk and can be knitted or crocheted, or even netted and have large, flowing, sometimes knotted and braided tassels at the ends. There is a long slit in the middle that admits your hand. The bag is opened and closed through a series of interconnecting sliding metal rings. The coolness of the metal slides across your fingers and strengthens their grip as they part open and slip inside the silk-lined opening that closes round the wound as soon as it is made.

If I were to make such a purse, I might line it with silk onto which has been embroidered the face of a beast. I could then thrill with girlish delight every time I dipped my hand into its throated den and managed to withdraw it unscathed.

Brief though my sight of it was, I can sketch in detail the miniature portrait of Benjamin Franklin that I observed. It was remarkable in its precision and even more remarkable in the effect achieved by the peculiar representation of his hair. Virtually straining against the borders of its frame is this huge cloud of shaded white hair that surrounds the face and spills into the very corners of the board as its disappears from sight under the frame. The hair lifts off at the temples and wings outward and upward all around. It connects the face, held here to earth, with a world outside of it. It is as if the force of that unseen world has reached down its hand, opened a passage to this world, and closed its fingered grasp upon the hairs of his head, pulling them through the slits at the edge of the frame.

I have been back to the Louvre, this time by myself. I left the children with Ada, the governess, despite their spirited protests. We spent yesterday at Notre Dame and will be leaving Paris so very shortly that I am keenly aware that if I do not steal the time now I will miss this opportunity completely. I wanted to return especially to view again a casket of the most richly worked kind that my brief glimpse of which assured me issued from a truly extraordinary hand. It is from the sixteenth century and must have been used to hold only the most precious of letters or jewels. It is carved from ebony of the deepest hue and formed into the shape of a cross. Across the horizontal piece is inlaid an elaborate garland of jewels: emeralds, rubies, diamonds. Down the vertical line of its form run parallel lines of inlaid ivory; these lines terminate by joining together into a tightly coiled form that fills the lower corners of the bottom of the cross. This vessel is large. It is a full two-feet high and a good foot-and-a-half wide. I know the skill and the time it must have taken to inlay it so well.

But it is the carving that surrounds all the ivory and the jewels that is truly remarkable. There is not a fraction of an inch that is untouched. Every space on the entire piece has been carved into a virtually endless series of tiny rosettes. I cannot describe adequately the texture that it is; I could not feel it myself for this is kept inside a glass enclosure. I can only imagine how sharp it must have felt when your fingers grasped it to lift off its cover. And the odd sensation created by this large, once-solid piece of wood now deliberately incised in such a painstaking manner. It seems that it must have been deprived of much of its substance—so much seems to have been carved away. And yet this cannot be so. It has stood strong enough to last these centuries. I imagine my fingers cutting each rosette and then re-cutting it to achieve exactly the tightness of curl my mind's eye requires. Then I think of the time and the care and the devotion that went into its making, and then into the hundreds of others so lovingly and precisely carved by these same hands. And it is here that I feel the devotion of faith in a way that I cannot feel under the huge, cavernous, carved arches of cathedrals. It is here, in the picture of the hands that carved this casket into a receptacle made fit to receive the most precious of objects, that I witness the hand of my faith.

Lizzie

Squaw pussy is what he has taken to calling me. I laugh. There's worse things in the world, I tell him. I tell him this too. Next time you come near me, you'll find out what a squaw's pussy is all about.

Sophia

Oh how I wish I had thought to pack the gloves that Elizabeth sent me from Madrid. Even the sounds of that city's name thrill me. Ma-drid, Ma-drid, Mad-rid, Mad-rid, I say, over and over, feeling a rushing, tingling down my back. I swear I can feel it in the center of my spine. These gloves are exquisite. They are of white kid, kid so soft and smooth that when you touch it you'd swear you were stroking the softest of down. They stretch so tightly over your hand that every vein is visible. Over the entire length of the glove are painted wavy green lines. At the wrists are triple bands embroidered with tiny garlands of flowers. These are not New England flowers. They are fervid, and spicy, and of the deepest hues. Dead in the center of the back of each hand is a black medallion, outlined with gold thread. Inside is a finely detailed picture of a man presenting a gift to a woman who is seated under a tree. If you flex your hand, you can almost see the woman reach up and take the box from the hand that proffers it. If you flex your hand hard enough you can imagine her opening the box and disappearing into its vast interior. Then again, you can relax your hand and keep her safe under the tree.

-Yellowbird-

Yellowbird repeats the center design. There are a series of vertical diamonds, the outsides of which are done in a zigzag stitch and are blue and red. The inside field is yellow and brown for which she uses line stitching, always careful to keep her quill moist with her saliva. Her stitches are small, even, nearly invisible. When she runs her hand over the surface, she feels only the smooth, flowing whole of each little mound.

Yellowbird hums all day and all night. She knows John Hawkridge Hitchcock is in the grove, stuck in its perimeter. She knows, too, that he will not find her. She is safe, as she has been these thousands of years.

Sophia

I have had a nightmare from which I sometimes feel that I can never awaken. A number of years ago a friend described to me in great detail a painting she had seen while abroad. It was the image of a woman, dressed in elaborate fashion and with many wavy and ruffled petticoats, swinging and looking off to her side. Down in the lower right corner was the figure of a man, crouched into a position from which, when she passed overhead, he could look up into the center of her legs as she whirl-winded past. I remember having this picture come into my mind this night, though I do not know why it should have occurred to me. Some time later I was awakened with such force and trembling that I hurried down to the parlor, being careful not to disturb my husband as I left, and have sat to attempt to write down as accurately as possible the vision that has presented itself to me.

I became the figure on the swing and could feel the wind wave around me with each pass, could feel the rushed air wave over my face as I lifted first one leg and then the other. This lasted some time—long enough that I was spun as high as the very tree tops, seeing myself almost move out of the frame. I was in the swing and I was the figure crouched in the corner, looking up, underneath. Those eyes became leeches that propelled themselves out of my face and into my legs and began to suck with a sigh that mocked the wind around me. I reach up, pull them off, and I crouch again, watching the blood flow from overhead.

These words and the writing of them have a power that I do not understand. All I know is that I must put this pen down. If I do not, I will be bled dry.

Lizzie

Sophia told me that once pressed into the page, words remain. So, too, desire. Such is her faith.

My faith has sent me a vision. Her blood is white and black and red and she wears quilled moccasins so fine that no one can hear her when she walks the earth. At her side she carries a huge knife in a quill case so fine that no one notices when her hand withdraws.

Sophia

It has taken us far longer than we had anticipated to arrange our departure from Rome, but we have managed to leave it behind. We have been in London and are now in Redcar, a truly beautiful village on the coast. The sands are shiny and white; the water often deep, reflective blue. But I am not well. My fatigue is something infinite.

We are at home again. Neither Elizabeth nor Mary visit often, though Lizzie still does write, though not often and not at length. Even though my husband has been able to work, he broods often. He has mentioned that the one thing he liked about Italy were the towers that so frequently were a part of houses there. In them, you had the feeling of being above the filthy life below. So I have set myself to a project. I am going to remodel Wayside so that he has a tower study. If he can sit high enough in the tower, maybe he will forget the filth at his feet. Perhaps, then, he can find some peace.

I find that I simply can no longer wear the newest fashion—the crinoline and the gored skirt with but one flounce at the bottom since the crinoline itself gives sufficient width to the bottom of the skirt. It does have its advantages. You can walk ever so much more comfortably since you do not have those stiff horsehair petticoats scratching your legs. And the skirted bottom half of myself is so very wide, that it makes it seem that I indeed have a waist again. But I did have difficulty ascending or descending the stairs; the skirt is so wide and full that it obscures your vision of what is literally in front of you. It is most odd that I do not recall ever having had difficulty abroad, where this has been the fashion for years. But that difficulty alone probably wouldn't have been sufficient reason for me to put aside such fashionable dress. But as I was trying to negotiate the stairs I had this image of my bottom half as one gigantic mushroom fungus that had arisen from the ground and was pushing my top half up through the roof. If I could have seen myself break through the roof and fly, it would have been one thing. But all I could see was the top of me sticking out of the top of the house with the ballooned lower half of me wedged tight below. And then I saw my husband come home, and look up to the top of the stairs to discover fat legs dangling in space, enveloped by petticoats formed into a cage by circles of whalebone. So this is what it has come to—a beached whale, I thought. And to think that I was making fun of Elizabeth. Oh well, if I am a whale, and I am to be beached, then let it be near the water, with body dressed in a manner more natural to my shape. Let me not cut so ludicrous a figure as to be a pitiably narrow top half sticking out of a bottom half literally as wide as a house.

I cannot remember if I thought that he smiled or sneered when he looked up. But it is no matter, I guess.

Lizzie

As he ran toward me, I cringed. He scooped me up, twirled me around, then swirled me outward and back, and sang and danced me around the entire house. He laughed, smiled, said he really did love me, that he was so sorry for everything always, and then he sang and he danced and I threw back my head and opened my mouth and breathed hard and long, filling myself with enough air that I wanted to burst. I laughed till I cried and then I laughed some more. I could feel his tender fingertips in my back, stroking and kneading and then I could feel them at my waist, circling round and holding tight and lifting me ever so high toward the ceiling and then the window. I could feel the surge of air from the open pane on the third floor of our house as I saw the mountain outside, that part of the mountain that looks sometimes like a whale and sometimes like a human face when you are three stories high. And then he twirled me round the edges of the room and then into the center and then back toward the window where he scooped me up in his arms, his hands under my knees. "I could throw you right through that goddamned window, my dear, anytime I wanted to," he whispered as he motioned throwing me to my doom.

Herman is at such dis-ease, poor bastard. The stupid beast eats at his own heart. But I cannot let pity sway me. If I do, he'll bite harder than ever. And I'll have to bite harder back.

In this first paragraph I sound way too much like Sophia.

But by the second, I'm back.

Sophia

The study is taking longer than I had hoped. Yet another of the workmen has left to join the Union Army. I am afraid that it will be increasingly difficult to find workers. Prices have begun to escalate so that I am afraid how much it will actually cost. I am glad, though, that we bought the clock just when we did. I have heard that the price has risen five dollars in the last week alone. It is a fine piece, with spires at either end of the central steeple, and a dial painted round with roses. On the glass front, through which is visible its brass pendulum, the roses are repeated, in larger scale, and joined by all manner of other blooms that wreathe around the perimeter before working their way toward the center. It chimes on both the hour and the half hour. I wind it every morning at eight, it having a thirty hour movement. I like to hear the grinding crunch of the springs being wound tight.

We did manage to find enough workers and the study was finally completed, though at ever so much more expense than we had anticipated. I am appalled by what has happened to prices; they seem to soar overnight. The excuse is always the same. We're told it will only get worse as the land moves deeper into conflict. So I guess I should be grateful that it is complete and cost only four times as much as originally planned.

But it is, alas, a failure, a very expensive failure. In the summer it is unbearably hot. In the winter, he shakes so with the cold that he cannot hold his pen. His study overlooks a meadow but the view brings no inspiration—or comfort. He is not well. Oh, he is truly not well at all. He has begun to assume a shape that frightens me. His chest is sinking and his stomach grows. He has a hunched look most days. He writes little and finishes less.

And it is a failure in another way. It is, of course, more fashionable now. It is high gothic style which is all the rage, with the turrets and all the gingerbread trim and the new windows with their crosshatched, diamond-shaped patterns. But the old and new forms have not married well. It is not the productive union that I had envisioned. It has become a horrible polygamy as it has been forced into a union with features not its own. Poor thing. It has had to assume a face that has nothing to do with its soul.

It is, indeed, a disfiguring presence. It hurts my eyes to see it so.

-Yellowbird-

"Motley Dog, old girl," Yellowbird laughs, "let's tell each other again how it came to be that all the tribes of the world paint their bodies."

Even before the First Time, Great Grandfather decided that he was going to give birth to all the peoples of the earth. Great Grandmother warned him that he would not be happy. But Great Grandfather insisted that he knew how to create the people of the world. He would make them different colors, so he could tell them apart and they could know where they belonged. He made a map of the world in his mind and made people to fit each part.

When he was finished he was not happy. They did not stay where he had placed them. Soon his world teemed with strange-colored intermixtures; sooner still his world gave way to wars as one color tribe moved into another color's territory.

Great Grandfather called the world's people together and said you should mark yourselves so that the others can read you. Let us all know, he pleaded, whether you are hunting or making war or coming in peace. Let us all know, he pleaded again, what color you really are since so many of you are so mixed together that I cannot tell what you are.

Some people make their marks permanent, burning colors into their flesh. Others use colors that fade or wash away; they have many different faces.

Yellowbird favors the ones who change. "Look at the stars Motley Dog," she says pointing upward. "Every night the sky has a different pattern. But if you look closely you can read the star signs and learn that each pattern comes again in a fixed time."

Yellowbird knows how to read the world. She understands its signs. Motley Dog reads well too. Mixed colors bring her joy.

Lizzie

We are in Manhattan, on Twenty-Sixth Street, though it does not matter. It would all be the same no matter if we had never left the mountains. His writing does not sell, has not sold these many years. He works at the Customs House, goes abroad to the inns with the men, and returns as haunted as ever. He swears the halls here have ghosts. These are not the same halls in which our son Malcolm shot himself but my husband swears he hears gunshots coming from the third floor, hour after hour, day after day. He cannot sleep; he fears the shots are aimed at him. He often squats in the corner, hands over his head, trembling. He cries, sometimes for hours. Worse yet, he whimpers, sometimes all night. The howls were better, I remind myself. I do not go to him.

I am convinced, though, that at night some beast does prowl past our door. I hear it lick its lips. I pray that I will find Lulu's animals at the end and not the jaws of this monster. But prayer does no good. His Christian God is no god for me.

I look to the stars but they don't answer here. The stars are different in the city, though. They are framed, boxed in by the buildings. Yet they seem more distant. There are no mountains here to set you closer to them. But that is a comfort too. So many stars dwarf you when your husband shoots your name through haunted halls.

Sophia

He keeps many notebooks—notebooks of many, many pages.. When he is in his study, the door is closed to me. But when he is not, both the door and the journals are open. I have often, especially while straightening and dusting the shelves, stood at his desk and perused a goodly number of pages. I did not expect such vitriol; I expect, though, that what he says about Margaret has something to do with what he doesn't write down about me. This is an ungenerous thought, I know. But his words before me are not only ungenerous—they seem to me unregenerate. And the pettiness, too. To call her strong and heavy and unpliable. I fancy for the moment that I would like to do a portrait of her as she appears in the now-eternal room somewhere beyond the borders of this world. She would have the same hairstyle that she had a decade ago—with the hair at each side of her head parted sharply so that, if looked at from the side-view, it forms a circle around each ear, leaving the entire ear completely visible and open.

Lizzie

Dear Lizzie: Oh God, Lizzie, I think I know the whole damned thing. Oh, I know the whole thing. Hawthorne got really drunk—the only time in his life, I believe, that he was ever so—and said strange, disturbing things. Not a story, exactly, but bits and pieces here and there; just enough for me to make out the whole. Almost like he confessed to the air, and I just happened to be there. Don't ever tell Sophia; it would kill her, poor dear. —Margaret

Margaret would have died if she really knew the whole story. As it is, she is dead now. The sea picks her clean; the waves slam and slam and slam.

I keep thinking of Hiram and his strip troops, the war he waged with pieces. And how he knew when to leave the field.

Sophia

I have been sitting and looking at a very recent photograph of myself. It does not have the effect I intended. I am seated in the chair with the carved crest at its back, sitting next to my marble-topped parlor table upon which rests a stack of books. I am wearing my long gold chain with my watch suspended from it. The watch is not pinned at my waist; the watch is held in my hand. But I am hunched over it, with a surprised, stricken look on my face. My lips are parted in a pursed laugh. I do not know what it is that wants to emerge from them. The black netted scarf which I draped over my head and gathered at the nape of my neck looks as if it hangs like a huge weight, weighing me down and bending me over at the waist. I am a hunched thing, bent over in pain, eyes narrowed to slits. It is as if I am on the edge of the seat, ready to spring forward, at the very verge of lifting myself into life. But I do not move. I am held there, rigidly, frozen forever.

I hold him shivering against me, again. His shiver cannonades through me, from temple to sole. I throb with his cold. I cannot warm him. Hell is not noise. It is not heat. Hell is a shivering, isolating self that cannot warm.

I must think of other things. Some Berlin wool has arrived and I am determined that I am going to cross-stitch a new piece for our parlor fire-screen. But every time I start the pattern I am dissatisfied and end the night unlooping all the knots that I have knotted. My fingers ache; my knuckles knot.

He has become so bloated that his head seems dwarfed now. And his legs and feet seem like slim reeds trying desperately to uphold the impending crash of a tidal wave. The pain gnaws from deep inside. I have no faith that he will be able to stand long.

A grayness more deep and leaden than any I can remember has seeped across the land. The only color which penetrates this is the blood that spills forth both north and south. Elizabeth does all she can for the wounded soldiers but she is painfully aware that she can offer nothing that can ease the physical pain. And how can the soul ever be eased if the leg to which it is attached is rotting with gangrene? She said that to smell their bodies makes one lose faith at times in the very notion of a soul anyway.

Maybe because of all this I have been thinking about a performance that I heard is to be given—or already has been given, I am not really sure. An actress—Menken is, I think, her name—is to play the lead role in an adaption of Byron's *Mazeppa*. She is going to play the lead role of the male military hero. It is all about a Polish military hero, I think. Byron's hero was male but all the advertisements make clear that he is to be played by a woman. Anyway, she is going to be strapped to the back of a horse and she will be ridden on a ramp that vaults across the audience and terminates on the stage. She is dressed in a flesh-colored costume so that she will give the appearance that she is naked. And it is as this—a woman dressed to appear like a nude man who is strapped on the back of a horse—that she figures the heroic welcome. This, to my mind, is not a pleasing image. My image of a heroic figure is not strapped to the back of the horse. My figure straps the horse with the shape of her open legs, unfettered with the need for costume. But surely it is or will be all the rage, I am sure. These sorts of theatrics have infected us.

There is a line that keeps recurring to me, although I cannot remember its author. There is a pain so sharply deep that the flesh it cuts does not bleed.

I do not know what is the matter with me. I have cut out the pattern for a dress; I have all the pieces done and all that remains is for them to be pieced together. But each time I take two pieces, lay them together face-to-face, I find myself utterly unable to begin the stitches that will join their backs together. I am utterly unable to begin to fashion the seam that will give them shared shape. I do not like anymore to look at these pieces. If I leave them, unsewn, but still atop one another, I imagine that they part their sides, the top flap curving upward, the bottom ever so slightly down, into a shape like lips. They part; they speak.

If I could collect all of my letters, it strikes me that I would have a journal of me that I released in bits and pieces over the years. What an interesting idea about publishing—it makes even the serial installments of novels seem like shallow, short things. But, alas, this can never be.

173

All of the letters I wrote to him before we were married he burned long ago. But if I were to collect what is left, I wonder what sort of me could be gathered on sheets framed by leather covers. What words would be incised upon my spine?

"Get my manuscript—now."

I could not believe my ears. "But, dear," I remonstrated, "you know this is our wedding night. Can't it wait until tomorrow?"

"Get it—now," he insisted.

"But please, dear," I pleaded.

"Now," he insisted again.

"Just not tonight—just this once, please?" I cried.

His face carried no emotion. He backed his way, slowly, intentionally, toward the door. He backed out, staring at me all the while, closed the door and locked it. He left me there for hours.

"Now, will you get it?" he roared, unlocking and opening the door with noise and fury.

I made no protest; there was no use.

I took up his manuscript. I walked to the middle of the room and lay it down. I then got on my hands and knees holding the manuscript as I read him his work. He came to me, knife in hand. He slashed my dress, ripped it from me. He rammed me from behind, slammed into me like he would split me in two. I kept reading the whole time.

Sophia

My husband is dead. I was not with him. He went on a journey to restore his health. But he was not alone. Franklin Pierce was with him. That is something I have always admired. They remained loyal to each other through it all, despite the criticism. So I am glad that he had someone at his side who cared deeply and well for him. But I know that he faced those final moments absolutely by himself, as we all will. I have not asked Franklin if there were any last words and Franklin has not volunteered any. I hope fervently that he will. But I am afraid to ask. I am afraid that there were none. The end was quick, though, and for that I am grateful. He could have suffered so much longer.

He has been buried, according to our wishes, at Sleepy Hollow. If I had Heathcliff's faith I would have kept the cover off. But, alas, I do not believe that what has ceased to flow in life can be resurrected in death.

But perhaps I should have more faith. After all, he is not Heathcliff and I am not Catherine. Our lives have not been lived upon the pages of a novel. Perhaps we can bleed into each other even with the covers closed.

-Yellowbird-

Yellowbird nudges Motley Dog; Motley Dog growls softly, rolls on her back, pawing the air. "Motley Dog, old girl," Yellowbird snorts, "that's a get-up-quick nudge." Motley Dog rolls over again. Gets to her feet. "I see a terrible thing about to happen. I don't want to watch it alone." Motley Dog rubs up against Yellowbird's ankle, licking her leg. Yellowbird is heartened; knows she will be able to stand what it is she has to see. She closes her eyes, empties herself, opens her heart.

"The time will come Motley Dog," Yellowbird begins, "when a strange hatchet-like blade will plummet to the earth. It will fall swiftly, terribly. As it falls, its metal blade will reflect light into a thousand tiny shards. Hard, sharp, shards of light everywhere. This strange and terrible blade will fall with great force; when it hits Porcupine in the middle of his back it will split him in two."

Motley Dog cringes, pulls closer yet to Yellowbird's leg. Yellowbird reaches down, pats her, rubs her back. "Don't worry, Motley Dog, old girl," Yellowbird assures. "This story starts bad but I don't think it ends the same way. But we'll see."

Yellowbird closes her eyes again, empties herself, opens her heart once more. It is a few minutes before the vision resumes; Yellowbird chides herself that she ought to know by now not to interrupt a vision since you don't know if it will ever get back to showing itself to you. But Yellowbird now begins again to see that hatchet fall into Porcupine's back. "The hatchet slices Porcupine right in two. His sides fall away from each other, away from the blade now stuck well into the earth. On either side, Porcupine's feet still quiver; his split tail still shivers. Blood runs fast from his divided body. Poor thing. His death is near."

Motley Dog whimpers, shakes. Yellowbird hangs her head as she

177

feels the creature's pain. "The blood is so thick it has buried the hatchet blade from view. So thick it seems impossible that a small creature could contain so much." Yellowbird is about to open her eyes, about to close her heart, fill herself with herself. "Oh, my. Oh, my. Great Spirits that be. Blood of every color shoots forth. Yellow, red, black, white. From Porcupine's half selves, blood of every color seeps into the earth. As it flows over the buried hatchet blade, the blade changes shape. It becomes a huge needle, with a large eye. The many-colored blood becomes many-colored threads. The threads find their way through the needle; the needle finds its way to the center of Porcupine's dual halves. Stitch by stitch, Porcupine is made whole. Stitches so fine that their scar becomes invisible under the quills atop Porcupine's back."

Motley Dog wags her tail, barks. Remembers herself as a young pup, teething on Yellowbird's blanket. Yellowbird opens her eyes, closes her heart, feels herself return to her breast. It is the way of the wise, she thinks. Even split in two, a whole self may yet emerge, hiding the deep scar that runs the perimeter of the body. Even bleeding to death, we can bind our torn selves together.

Sophia

I cannot sleep. I rise. I go to the attic to my trunk. I descend to the front parlor. I undress. I clasp the pearls around my neck; I have not worn them since the funeral. I arrange my veil. It is not the same body that I see in the looking glass. The veil is yellowed. The skin bears furrows. Through the veil I see a series of looking glasses. I see Don Fernando. He steps forth from his glass, the middle one, and steps into the front one where I sit in the parlor on Chester Street, canvas in hand. But he is right. I cannot recover this. I remove the veil, fold it carefully, lay it on the settee. I pause before the Staffordshire dogs on the mantel, amused by their fake ferociousness. I hold the music box my husband bought me but do not wind it; I do not wish to hear it sing. I light the lamp and let it burn, shadeless, for a moment. I climb the stairs. I dress.

I descend once more and stand in front of the looking glass, watching my earrings reflect patterns of flowered light. Six-sided stars seem to surround me. I see a series of parlors. And then I am in the mesmerist's portrait parlor. A figure steps out: whether it is the mesmerist or the figure in the painting I do not know. It is as if he were at my back; I reflect his reflection as he stares past me, beyond me. And then we are in my Manse studio that is also a parlor. I begin to paint. The looking glass becomes a transparent canvas that reflects no frame. I am looking out from my window, out into the Concord garden, past to the river and the ice-covered trees. Glass chandeliers, my husband called them. I look to the hills that frame the view. I want to stay in this parlor but cannot.

The looking glass is yet another reflective canvas. I see my mother before me, from the waist upward, black-dressed, red-hatted, uncorseted. She forms into a mountainous face, framed by gardens of fervid hues, spiced and spiked blossoms rising and forming the circumference of the glass before me that I now brush into shape. Strong, angular, sharp peaks align with spiked, spicy petals. I can almost smell the oranged hue as I build a series of brush-stroked slopes and crevices along each one. Other blossoms emerge, valleyed with folds and rippled with hues, riding astride the mountainous outline, fleshing depth to the scene.

A blue-black light emerges from the far right edge. The river, frozen, reflects the red-black forms that cover its sheeted surface. I hear Elizabeth and Margaret and Lizzie laugh. I see my brush stroke to life the truncated figure of a man whose eyes are the red-black forms that slide over the iced sheet of water, whose halo of hair encircles a named cry that can not reach its sound.

I now work slowly and carefully, erasing all visible strokes. I begin a lace border, making the new circumference widen to the edges just beyond sight. The bodkin appears. I take it in my timid hand and ribbon through the edges and I watch it sewn slowly shut.

I turn and climb the stairs. I take my unfeatured face in my hands. I rest my elbows on the sill of the leaded glass window on the landing. I finger my earrings, feeling the edges of each stone. I let my eyes retrace the geometric diamonds of metal frames that contour each piece, that hold together the shards of glass, not unlike the way metal wires shape into one the crystal fragments of a glass chandelier. I look out. The glass is clear, save for the ripples and bubbles that are in its nature. I look out to a world, wavy with life, pulsing through the tiny, circular bubbles. I stare, hard. The bubbles lose their firm edges; they are moss bud bubbles, dancing themselves onto the lawn and across the field and down to the river, skating over the frozen surface. The world is framed. The leaded panes hold tight. I will not get reflected beyond its borders.

I climb once more. My hand is on the deeply-engraved brass knob of the door. The door is carved from heart pine and embellished with a veneered pattern of flame-grained mahogany. I stare, hard. There is a face that meets me, reflected off the glossy varnish of its surface, which moves ever so slightly with the waving nature of the wood. I begin to rock with it, matching my breath to the warmth of its grain.

Lizzie

He has given me a book of poems. He calls it "Weeds and Wildings, Chiefly, With a Rose or Two." He swore he loved me, never meant to hurt me. He goes out, with the men, to the Inns, as always. When he returns he can barely stand. He cries, he bellows, "Lizzzzeeeeee, pleeee-ase." He swings at the air, fists tight, misses. He falls, passes out, perhaps even sleeps. Perhaps still desires. I will not harm him. There is no grace in that.

Lizzie Shaw Squaw left Manhattan at sunrise in April 1886. She took the train to Chicago, then a hired carriage to Quebec. From there a trapper with horses guided her to the Territories and from there to the Settlement. She had intended to make this last part of the journey alone but the trapper stayed with her to the Settlement. Lizzie loves his touch, soft as the moss. He asks her name; "Lizzie Shaw Squaw," she growls, softly.

When they reached the Settlement in June, Lizzie did set out alone, on foot, to retrace John Hawkridge Hitchcock's journey. Of course she could never find his exact path. That does not matter.

When she had walked for four days she stops. She carries with her a large beaded bag, embroidered with the face of a lion, mane large and wild. The lion is deep orange, his mane outlined in deepest black; the background is purple, magenta, and the brightest green. Out of this lion's mouth she withdraws a pair of moccasins and a knife case in which rests a large blade with a handle hand-carved in the shape of an eagle, accented with small diamonds shaped from mother-of-pearl. Lizzie still has one last stitch to complete in each moccasin and in the knife case. She wants to be on the open fields to make those last stitches.

She sits, cross-legged, and draws the last quills through her teeth. She flattens them well as she draws them through her fingers; she wants her fingers to glide over the surfaces, feeling only a seamless whole. She completes each stitch deliberately, slowly, perfectly. She feels a calm she has never before known.

Lizzie puts on the moccasins and stands up. She straps her knife to her side, licks her lips, feeling the red and black and white deepen in her eye. Knife at her side, with moccasined feet, she walks back, slowly, deliberately, with confident and silent step.

When she reaches the Settlement, the trapper is still there, waiting. She is not afraid of smooth sand; she need not marry. Lizzie Shaw Squaw, he calls her, soft as moss.

-Yellowbird-

Motley Dog is dead. Yellowbird cries. The zigzag furrows on her face are so deep and wide that her tears take hours to fall from her cheek. When they finally fall, she makes her way to the soup pot, slowly, painfully. She knows what she must do.

The pot is nearly empty but there is enough for one last meal and enough to dye that one last quill the deepest shade of all. She lets the quill simmer for hours. It must be dark enough to be the center. It will have to be deepest deep, she tells herself, to be the last stitch of all.

When it is deep enough, she drinks. She drinks slowly, ever so slowly. She must empty the pot, she knows; she will do so as slowly as possible.

She turns and retraces her steps, recalling the many thousands of times she has walked this path. Yellowbird keeps her eyes down. She walks more slowly than ever, trying to stay the moment when she must see what she must see, must do what she must do. She does not want to see Motley Dog, whose body has been split in two, and the unmolested blanket which she now must finish.

She comes to the edge of the blanket and lifts her head. She tells herself the time has come. She looks up and is amazed, thankful. The blanket is undone. The center is gone; it is unraveled. Wagging her tail is Motley Pup, snarling playfully as she unravels yet more of the blanket with her sharp, white teeth.

Yellowbird smiles, showing her smooth mound teeth and she begins to sing. Softly, soft as green moss, she sings. She knows now the pot is again full. She licks her lips. Yellowbird adds the deepest colored quill to the fistful she picks up, holds their barbed ends in her teeth, and pulls them smooth, taut, flat. She gives thanks as she watches Motley Dog's split body absorb into the earth.

She stitches, even, perfect, almost invisible stitches. Reds, browns, blacks, yellow, blues, all the colors of earth and sky, in shapes that do not end, under so many stars.

Printed in the United States
101795LV00002B/49-78/A